Essentially

Essentially

Essays by

RICHARD TERRILL

HOLY COW! PRESS
Duluth, Minnesota
2022

Author photograph by Linda Tse.

Cover photograph by Jerzy Durczak.

Book and cover design by Anton Khodakovsky.

Printed and bound in the United States.

First printing, Fall, 2022.

10 9 8 7 6 5 4 3 2 1

Library of Congress Cataloging-in-Publication Data

Terrill, Richard, 1953- author.
Essentially : essays / Richard Terrill.
Duluth : Holy Cow! Press, 2022.
LCCN 2022001766 | ISBN 9781737405139 (trade paperback)
LCGFT: Essays.
LCC PS3620.E767 E77 2022 | DDC 814/.6—dc23/eng/20220223
LC record available at *https://lccn.loc.gov/2022001766*

ISBN 978-1737405139

Holy Cow! Press projects are funded in part by grant awards from the Ben and Jeanne Overman Charitable Trust, the Elmer L. and Eleanor J. Andersen Foundation, The Lenfestey Family Foundation, The Woessner Freeman Family Foundation, and by gifts from generous individual donors. We are grateful to Springboard for the Arts for their support as our fiscal sponsor.

Holy Cow! Press books are distributed to the trade by Consortium Book Sales & Distribution, c/o Ingram Publisher Services, Inc., 210 American Drive, Jackson, TN 38301.

For inquiries, please write to: Holy Cow! Press, Post Office Box 3170, Mount Royal Station, Duluth, MN 55803.

Visit *www.holycowpress.org*

For John

Contents

Acknowledgements

Thanks to the editors of the following journals in which most of these essays originally appeared, always in a different form:

"Solstice" in *Brevity*.

"Yet Again to the Lake" in *Colorado Review*.

"On Hearing/On Listening" in *Missouri Review*.

"The World Away" in *Split Rock Review*.

"Trout Fishing: A Manifesto" in *River Teeth*.

"Who Was Bill Evans?" in *Crazyhorse*.

"Ozu's *Tokyo Story (1953)*" in *Great River Review*.

"Neighbors" in *South Loop Review*.

"Introduction to Film – Section One, Tuesday 6-9:35 p.m., Fall Semester, 1996" in *1966: A Journal of Creative Nonfiction*.

"The Baker Boys: A Fable" and "The Horn" in *Brilliant Corners: A Journal of Jazz and Literature*.

"Essentially" in *Laurel Review*.

"Two Stories" (excerpt, as "Spring Creek") in *Kestrel*.

Thanks to the many readers who helped shape this writing, including Bronson Lemer, Kris Bigalk, Lynette Reini-Grandell, Don Morrill, Lisa Birnbaum, Bob Neumiller, and my past students in the graduate nonfiction workshop at Minnesota State, Mankato. I know there are others I've neglected to include on this list, especially for the older pieces. This is due to a deficient memory, not a lack of gratitude.

Thanks to editors who made suggestions for cuts and changes to earlier versions: Stephanie G'Schwind, Brett Lott, Dawn Morano, Evelyn Somers, Joe Mackall, Rebecca Lanning, Jim Perlman, Christine Stevens. Thanks to Dinty W. Moore for including "Solstice" in *The Truth of the Matter: The Art and Craft in Creative Nonfiction*.

Special thanks to Kara Balcerzak and Sarah Johnson, whose close reading and insightful suggestions on most of these essays made this book possible. You are essential!

"I think of it as being different kinds of music for different purposes. I hope that it's varied, and that it all sounds like me despite the variety."

—*Aaron Copland*

"The interest, the pastime, was to learn if there had been any divinity shaping my ends and I had been building better than I knew.... I had given up convictions when young from despair of learning how they were had."

—*Robert Frost*

I

THE WORLD
AWAY

SOLSTICE

"LIFE USED TO BE FUN," MY MOTHER SAYS A FEW DAYS BEFORE HER EIGHTY-ninth birthday. "Now it's shit."

It's hard to argue with her. Her memory is such that she asks me questions and by the time I answer, she's forgotten what she's asked. Our conversations take on an Abbott and Costello circularity. Suddenly disagreeable, she starts every sentence with "but." She no longer remembers my father, twenty years gone, and calls me by my brother's name.

"You just have to get out of bed and start your routine," I tell her. It's a lame proposition, I know.

"Why?" she asks.

Her contradictions, out of character for the person she used to be, are now the most rational feature of her discourse.

"I just want to be somewhere where I can help someone," she says.

She will never help anyone again, not even herself.

"I'm trying to be a person."

I walk her down to the lunchroom of the nursing home and sit with her next to her roommate "What's-Her-Name." Six months older than my mother, roommate Mabel has a broken knee that will now never heal, and a mind as cloudless as a mid-June day.

"When we got the farm, I cleared sixty acres of rocks," Mabel tells me. "Sixty acres…. But I loved it."

"This?" Mabel adds. "It's a hell of a life. But as long as I have my wits about me, I'll get by."

I know that Mabel is referring to my mom, and I'm thinking Mabel needs someone to point to who's worse off than she is. Maybe we all need that.

After lunch I leave the nursing home and drive for the woods. I've forgotten my fishing gear back in the city, but on Audie Lake I paddle my kayak on a day that's a poster for Wisconsin in early summer. Wild irises are in bloom wherever sun hits the shoreline. Water lilies. The lake with many bays and inlets I can explore. There are no cottages; there is no development to mar the shore. There are two skiffs fishing, some kids' laughter from a campsite out of view, a mother bald eagle tending her nest on a dead tree, wary of my little boat. Otherwise, only me. I drink two cans of beer in the sun and get delightfully toasted. I'm happy to forget who I am, one week before solstice, that midpoint. It will be the longest day, but the hottest weather comes in July.

I load my kayak atop my car for the drive home. There in the sand of the parking lot is a painted turtle, just more than the size of my hand. She doesn't move, though I could touch her with my paddle. Could kill her. Except I love turtles, love all creatures of the lake and its shore.

What is she doing here, seeing me, yet not moving away? Is she lazy, like me, avoiding something, enjoying something else? No, she's laying eggs. On this one day when something in the water or the air or herself tells her it's time.

She makes a kicking motion to cover the hole she's dug, then ambles off, her shell pieces of a puzzle, black lined by orange, flash of orange from her underside. A yellow line along each cheek. Her legs ancient skin, sinuous. She can smell the lake and knows which way to go.

She's crawling through a parking lot, so I step behind her to quicken her pace. I follow her all the way back to the water, which she crawls into the way someone tired might crawl into bed. She is beautiful to me. There is no way those eggs will ever hatch, ever bring forth life.

Heading out of the woods and on my way home too, six more times I stop my car, hurry turtles out of the sand, in the middle of the gravel road, before they're run over by some driver who doesn't care.

The Horn

A PIANO PLAYER AND I DO JAZZ SERVICES FOR LIBERAL CHURCHES. That sounds unusual, but there's quite a bit of work, and we enjoy the gigs because people listen to us more closely on Sunday morning in church than they do in bars or restaurants on Saturday night. It's a circuit, mostly small churches without full-time ministers, and we play for each congregation about once a year, when we've worked up a new program. I play the saxophone.

Bruce was the worship leader for a tiny Unitarian church in the suburbs—so small, never more than twenty in the room, that they met not in a sanctuary, but in a fifties-era strip mall storefront. Every year I wondered how they kept the church going. But it was a pleasant bunch, so here we were again.

When we arrived to set up, this was a couple of years ago now, Bruce had some news for me. The saxophone that he'd told me about, that had belonged to his father, and that I said last year I would like to see, he remembered to bring today. If I liked, I could use it today for the service.

"It's a great horn," Bruce said.

The truth was I had no memory of hearing about this saxophone twelve months before, much less having said I wanted to try it out. No way was I going to do a gig on a strange horn. Every horn, even every great horn, plays a little differently—different notes are sharp or flat, even the pearls on the keys meet the player's hands at different angles. To perform on someone else's axe would be something like running a race in someone else's shoes. Or maybe in someone else's pajamas.

"Ok, fine," I said, "let me blow some tunes on it after we're done."

How often the truth is the lesser of our concerns. Call it being polite, avoiding the issue, whatever. Bruce was the nicest of fellows, a retired lawyer who had ended his career as a mediator in divorce cases—trying to dial down the tensions, I imagined. I didn't want to offend, because though I didn't know Bruce well, he clearly was the kind of guy other people would call "a true gentleman." Soft spoken, seemingly interested in everything, he led this little group of secular humanists by example, it seemed.

So that was the extent of my interest in Bruce's saxophone—not wanting out of hand to say no to his offer. My own tenor sax I got in college, paid about one twentieth of what it's worth now. I had been playing it for forty-five years and counting. The horn and I had been through a lot together: jazz festivals, rowdy bars, weddings, even a couple stints living overseas. At one point I quit music and put the horn aside for ten years, but when I took it up again, it played well. And eventually, I played well again, too. I play mostly on the weekends, of course—and for Unitarians on Sunday mornings—and none of us weekend players were doing this for the money.

Over the years, more than once, friends who were players asked to try my sax, and their response was usually, "Nice horn. Want to sell it?" It was a Paris Selmer Mark VI, the Cadillac of horns, made the last year before Selmer stopped the line and introduced their said-to-be inferior Mark VIIs.

But Mark VI, Mark VII—that's shoptalk, and I'm anything but a shop kind of guy. I don't do well with any machines—power drills, car engines, computers, clarinets. The real reason I never took up the offers and sold my horn was that if I did, I'd have to go out and look for another one. It never quite seemed worth the trouble. A lot of sax players are horn geeks, in love with the mechanism as much as the music it produces. For instance, Jeff, a player and instrument repair man I know, has such a large collection of saxophones that, as he puts it, "if someone wants to blow the same model of horn that Lester Young used on 'These Foolish Things,' or Johnny Hodges used on 'Prelude to a Kiss,' I can lend it to him." This is an advanced case of the disease, to be sure, but the infection itself is a common one in the saxophone brotherhood. I say brotherhood because while there are more and more women in jazz, I imagine this machine passion remains kind of a guy thing. But I'm not that guy. I can't imagine the hassle. In fact, if I'd trained as a vocalist, no machine involved, I might have been perfectly happy. Maybe happier. As for saxophones, I was much more interested in the music that came out of them than I was in knowing the exact ways those sounds were made.

✷

After the gig, Bruce brought out the case that held the horn. I wanted to try it quickly and get home in time for lunch. "It's a Paris Selmer," Bruce said, (well, I hope so, I thought) "serial number in the fifty-five thousands." (Serial numbers are another geek thing. Some numbers are supposedly better than others. I could never remember the serial number on my horn.) "You remember I told you my father worked in a music store and played out on the weekends." (I didn't remember.)

"This was my father's horn," Bruce said again.

From the sound of his voice, it would be clear to one who knew him that Bruce was excited to show me the horn. But Bruce was not one to evince excitement. Instead there was a warm, measured look about him, ever the conciliator. What one thought was not necessarily better than what another thought. Open. Very Unitarian. I can only describe his demeanor as welcoming, though welcoming of what or to whom I couldn't say for sure, seeing him as I did only once a year. Probably welcoming to all.

"I've kept the horn for years, rarely played it. Mostly it sits in the closet. The horn plays too beautifully to be sitting in a closet. It needs to be in the hands of a great player."

"Well," I replied without missing a beat, "if I can find you a great player, I'll let you know...."

And to myself I wondered if Bruce knew enough about saxophones to be any judge of these matters.

"Look, even the case is in great shape."

It was at this point I realized Bruce was clearly trying to sell me his saxophone—*his father's saxophone*. I found out later that Bruce had gone back to lawyering work after an unplanned medical expense. I wondered then if he needed the money. But at this point I was thinking about my wife's duck noodle soup for lunch and a football game on TV.

"I'm sure we can agree on a price that we both think is fair," Bruce said.

Price? I opened the case and saw the horn resting in its velour cradle, like some rare artifact or jewel. There was only a slight smell of old brass and moisture about it, no mold, so the closet in which it resided had not been dank or closed up tight. The lacquer on the horn was deep and consistent, a rich gold. But I've seen players blow horns that looked like they'd spent years hanging on a garage wall that sounded fine, and other horns that looked vintage, yet were uncompromising in their stiff insistence on having it their way, not yours—like a disagreeable old man, something I hoped not to turn into. Appearance is not the best measure of age. I'd learned that much.

The lacquer on the horn was original—which added to its value on the marketplace. The horn had a blue plastic label across the front of the bell, the kind with stick-um on the back, that people used to make from label guns. "Thane Peck," it read. To my eyes, the only blemish.

I assembled the saxophone as I would any other, as I had my own horn for forty-five years, slid off the mouthpiece from my Paris Selmer to the neck of its elder cousin. I was well warmed up from playing the gig. I blew a few notes, I can't remember what, but probably just something from a d Dorian scale, which lies naturally on the sax.

My response to just those five or six notes was audibly, *oh my god*, and inaudibly, *I've missed this all my life....*

Most times our machines reflect our faults and flaws (some go sharp in the high register; on others the low notes don't speak.) Thankfully I can't know and thus can't say how much playing those first few notes on Bruce's father's horn was like discovering after one kiss with someone else that you have been married to the wrong person all of your life.

On this lovely old saxophone, every key, every note agreed with every other—no arguments involved. The horn was telling me to simply relax, that if I just did my share, it would see to everything else. It was experienced, broken in. Don't fight, don't adjust or compensate. Moderate. Make the air, make the air move. No, not perfection, but not worry about imperfection. It was so quickly clear.

It's probably no surprise that I knew right away I had to have the saxophone, and I pretended to be unsure about that fact for a week—only because I knew Bruce had no idea of what this horn was truly worth. He knew only what it was worth to him, upon which no dollar figure could be affixed. It had been his father's horn.

I knew he wouldn't ask the right price for the horn. By which I mean I knew he wouldn't ask enough money for it.

No surprise either that soon enough I bought the horn. But before I bought it, I took it to my own instrument repairman in town, one of the best in the country. It was no surprise that when he opened the case, his eyes betrayed an excitement that Bruce never would have expressed. And no surprise that he would say..., no exclaim, *this is a rare find!* In the future when I took the sax in to him for maintenance, he refused to charge me for his work.

Neither is it surprising that like the good Unitarian liberals that we were, Bruce quoted a price for his father's horn, and I said no, that I wouldn't pay it, and insisted on offering more. And then we reverse bargained until we agreed on a figure we were both less unsatisfied with. Deal.

✻

I've never believed that truth is stranger than fiction, but some events in life test that theory: that Bruce would suffer a stroke only a few months later, that by the time I got around to inquiring about a visit to him in rehab, he had died. That in the days before I was to play his father's saxophone at his memorial service, his daughter asked me, would you also please tell the story of my grandfather's saxophone?

The small family gathered for the service, as well as many, many friends— who due to their number meant that the event had to be held in a church much larger than Bruce's storefront. "...The truth was I had no memory of hearing about this horn twelve months before, much less having said I wanted to try it out...," I began, and as I spoke, a warm, welcoming air rose about the room.

Afterwards at the reception, people came up to me to tell me how much the story of the saxophone meant to them, and they told me their own stories about Bruce and their connection to him, almost as if I were family myself, or a lifelong friend. They couldn't know that they knew Bruce far better than I did. I was simply a guy who played the same horn as he did, the same horn as his father had.

I thought back to my own father's funeral, more than thirty years before. I remember being consoled that he'd had so many friends who came to pay respects. And then shortly after, feeling a little miffed that he was gone and they were still all here to say goodbye.

※

"Thane Peck," read the blue plastic label affixed to its bell. How strange to put a name on your horn, as if on the labels of the tee shirts your mother was sending with you to summer camp. I left the name there for a time, even after I had played a couple of gigs—marvelously, near perfectly—on the horn. And when I did tear off the label, it left one of those ghost marks on the bell, like when you pull scotch tape from the back of an old photograph.

My first Paris Selmer saxophone, my machine of forty-five years, sits in a closet now. It's too beautiful to stay there. And in the end it's *only* a machine, a means to a musical end. I will let it go for a price less than I could get for it, and I expect no argument, one way or the other, with whoever buys it. Surely it needs to be in the hands of a great player. Or better, a young player—who knows, maybe a great-player-to-be?

When I find one, I'll let myself know.

Yet Again to the Lake

I'M TRESPASSING ON THE LAKEFRONT LOT THAT MY FAMILY SOLD FIF-
teen years ago. There's a building there now that looks to be almost new,
but really only the windows and window frames are new. And the siding,
the added bedroom, the roof, the indoor bathroom, the modern kitchen,
the redone foundation, the new plumbing, wiring, and heating.

Everything else is original.

When I was trespassing here last year, the guy in the next cottage down
the shore said that the people we sold the cottage to tore everything away,
but kept the frame rather than rebuild from the ground up. That way they
could grandfather in the code violations, especially the one that forbids sit-
uating any structure this close to the water. It's nice to be right on the lake.

Shading my eyes to peer in each of the new windows, I see the shiny
bathroom in pastel shades (our outhouse still stands at the edge of the property, near the swamp.) I see the kitchen with porcelain double sink and
new Formica countertops. There's a full-sized refrigerator freezer, not the
Hotpoint antique that had been in my parents' apartment when they were
married during the War. There's new laminate flooring—it's even clean. A
microwave on a wooden cart.

The knotty pine paneling and interior walls are the same. I'm wondering but can't see if there are still holes in the wall where the knots fell out.
As kids, my brother and I could spy from one bedroom to the next through
these holes, or stick a finger through a hole and risk the guy in the next room
grabbing it and not letting go.

I suppose the new owners didn't know what to do with the privy, used
forty years. I try the door, but there's a lock on it now. A decorative plate with

a Janus face is nailed to the front. The plate looks two directions at once, but can't see anything either way, as far as I can tell. I look in the back window of the privy, and see they still store stuff in there, though I can't see just what. We stored there the springed-fish-holder-for-scaling-fish (what else to call it?) that my grandfather concocted, which now hangs in my garage. And a rickety grill on which, when one side was loaded with chicken over the coals, my mother had to put a small rock for balance on the other side to keep the food from tipping into the fire. When we painted the buildings on our lot, not a season sooner than we absolutely needed to, as a kid I was assigned to paint the back of the privy, being thought too young for a more responsible job. Now the paint job back there looks as fresh and neat as the one on the cabin. I find our old kitchen sink dumped back behind the privy, at the edge of the wetlands that border the property, what we used to call the swamp. I like it that, despite how new everything looks, the current owners are still dumping stuff behind the privy.

In the yard is evidence of a septic system. There's a new brick fire pit, landscaping, a gas grill. One willow tree my dad planted is still alive in front by the lakeshore, though the main trunk of it has died and been cut away, just fronds of green arcing from a high stump. These new people also managed to get some pines and a spruce and a red maple to grow down by the water, where we never could. For years, all through my childhood, my dad pushed wheelbarrows of sand down there to build up the shore, ours the lowest spot on the lake. But except for the weedy willows, nothing ever took for us. The new people have put in tons of fill, no doubt using a more efficient means of transport than one small, late middle-aged guy with a rusty wheelbarrow. What they've done is probably illegal, since the cottage stands next to a designated wetland—AKA the swamp. I know that the DNR surveys lakeshore from airplanes and will pinch people who fill in low spots next to official wetlands.

Even with all the rain lately (and how familiar does that phrase sound in vacation country?), the driveway has only a few small puddles. The new people must have filled in the driveway too, since in our day the two tire tracks would flood and the brown water would splash up on the sides of our

'63 Chevy station wagon when we pulled in. In the years before that, the brown water splashed up on the sides of our '60 Plymouth station wagon. Before that, on the sides of our 1950 Dodge Meadowbrook sedan. To make a driveway wide enough to haul in their big speedboat, the new owners cut down the hemlock trees where I used to play, in my woods.

The top of the nearest big pine is also gone—some kind of disease that had set in before we sold. Once my Uncle Virgil made a big and beautiful wooden sign for our cottage and hung it up at the road: "Two Pines," he called the place, after the two white pines on our double lot—the tallest trees on the whole lake. (Now there are one and a half pines.) We drove up one weekend—after Virgil and Aunt Vivian had been staying at the cabin for a week—and we saw the bold new sign hanging at the foot of the soggy driveway. Quite a surprise. Our place had a name, and a grand sign— maybe two feet by three, cut jagged along the edge to give it an outdoor look, painted deep brown with white lettering and a recessed painted image of a blue lake with two green sentinel pines. For years, people driving the curve at our place slowed down to admire the sign...and then their gaze turned to the tacky little yellow shack visible through the trees.

We took down the sign each winter, stored it in the privy with all the other stuff, but after a few seasons' weathering it became too heavy for the cross pole from which Virgil had hung it. Finally, the pole broke in half, and in the following years the sign never made it out of storage. Now it's in my brother's basement, a sign designating a place that no longer exists.

An hour or so ago, when I arrived back at the lake to skulk around and feel sorry for myself, the first things I noticed were the red pines that my father planted along the road with Uncle Virgil. There are more than twenty of them and now they are all are at least fifty feet tall, reaching high above the power lines, all beautiful. My Uncle Tom (who wasn't really an uncle, a complicated story like most family stories are), had helped with the plant- ing. Except that he hadn't. Tom and Dad had put in the red pines at the spot our woods ended and our open land near the road began. By the end of the next year, every one of those trees had died. Dad didn't know why. But that next year, he and Virgil replanted. Dad never told Tom that these trees weren't the same ones. Once a year during a summer weekend visit, Tom admired their new and steady growth.

*

I decide once again that this year will be the last time I trespass at our old cottage. I figure out that that's what I've been looking for on this trip today: the reason never to come back. For what do I hope to gain? Jar some memory heretofore lapsed? Indulge my overdeveloped sense of melancholy? It's all folly.

At what point did the future cease to be better than the past? The moment before my oldest memory? The beginning of my capacity for reflection? Until the mid-nineteenth century, nostalgia like mine was treated as a disease, thought sometimes to be fatal. Among soldiers at war, it was thought to have occurred in epidemics, especially when the armies were losing battles.

Over the years, nostalgia (from the Greek nostos, "to return home," and algos, meaning "pain") began to be seen not as a longing for a home, for a place lost to soldiers or traders. But as a longing for a lost time. In this more modern light, it became a disease of the mind, not a pathology. The phrase "incurable nostalgia" became a redundancy. Perhaps I'm trespassing today to question the logic of this revision, to test if one can feel the loss of a good place as sharply as the loss of an idealized time. Perhaps we can't grieve the loss of a time without also feeling the loss of the place with which it's identified. Or I can't.

Giving up nostalgia means recognizing we must live in a world that is much larger than our own concerns. Like Janus, wear a face that can look in more than one direction.

*

My earliest memory is set not at the house where I grew up in the city, not the neighborhood school I attended, but at the cottage. I'm standing near the back door, near the dirt and gravel driveway. I'm interested in its puddles. It's fall, and we're wearing lots of clothes. My family is there, and my cousin Jimmy, who never seemed like a cousin to me since he was an adult. For some reason I run toward the lake, the front yard. I guess I want to see what's there. The front porch that my dad had insisted be added to the cottage before he would sign the purchase agreement, that porch is still being built. Later and for years, the hastiness with which this porch was added will be a sore point. Squirrels will nest in the attic and chew holes in the ceiling, peer down at us while we sleep out there on warm nights. The roof will leak and rain will plop into metal pails and wash tubs we set out on the rotting floor. The warped doors won't close, and the long windows won't open.

But in this oldest memory the porch is just being built. It must be 1956, and I'm barely three years old. I remember feeling far away, out there alone by the lake, maybe fifteen adult steps from where the others are standing and talking in the back yard of the cottage. I look at the unfinished structure of the porch, the floorboards laid on the frame, and its incomplete nature frightens me, as if it's something I shouldn't see. Maybe it's like seeing someone in their underwear, the immodest beams and joists. Or maybe I know that this work has been done by other men, not by my father, who has no talent for carpentry; thus I have no call to be here.

Next I look toward the lake, and the sky gray with dense clouds. There is something other out there, a landscape outside of my body, unpeopled and thus alien, exciting. I turn and run back toward the driveway, towards family and safety.

That's it. Not even a story, hardly a picture. Just some boards lying on an unenclosed floor, and fall coolness in the air, me running awkwardly in too many clothes. A little trip away from civilization and back again.

In a later memory, a scene repeated many times, I'm lighting a fire in a small cave I've dug in the sand pile a few steps from the cottage door. The cave is the size of both my hands. My parents trust me and allow me to build the little fire. My dad is using the sand in the large pile to fill in at the shore of the lake, to make it less swampy there so we can swim, so he can grow trees to shade the front of the cottage. Every weekend he wheels load after load of sand down to the water, and by the end of the season, the shore has risen a little higher. But somehow, by the next spring the ground is just as wet, the sand washed into the lake or somehow disappeared. The forget-me-nots my mother likes still bloom along the shore. When you step there the water squeezes out over the toes of your shoes. A pace or two offshore, the lake bottom is still the black muck of dead leaves. We still can't swim at our place. And so the hauling process starts again.

I'm too young, too little to help. It's evening now, anyway, and work is done. The family is indoors after eating, with the little black and white TV on, a cottage extravagance. I start my fire in the sand with a few briquettes from the tippy grill on which my mother cooked supper. I pile small twigs on the coals and the flames reach out from my sand cave, stretching for air. I warm my hands and wonder at the sides of the cave growing black with soot. I might dangle an army man by a wire into the flames, watch his plastic features melt. I might squat there like an animal on its haunches, into the evening and night, fascinated, not minding the cooling air or the mosquitoes. The fire is mine, as is the sand cave, the mown perimeter around the cottage. Parents and brother are inside, black and white sound from the TV. This fascination with the danger of fire, its heat, and the chill of the June evening, and the coming stars and the frogs' music from the swamp next to our lot—one might expect from this a story of some flame that got away and burned a forest, a story of childhood guilt and drama. But there is none of that. So little really happens in the lives of most of us, and my boyhood Friday nights are no exception. I am simply alone with my fire, and soon I will go inside to be with others, because they are family. It's like coming in from some wild place, the spinning out of an innate need.

The stars are out now, and the peepers. I pull up the hood on the sweatshirt that bears the name "Norwood School." Before bedtime I will come back outside to go to the privy and look to see the red embers in my sand.

In his signature essay "Once More to the Lake," E. B. White writes about the summer cottage of his boyhood in Maine. "It is strange how much you can remember about places like that once you allow your mind to return into the grooves that lead back. You remember one thing, and that suddenly reminds you of another thing." I'm less interested than White in the process of remembering; I'm interested in the results, the place recalled, and maybe the people we were then, and why I think I would like to have it and them back from time to time, like a book I could take off of a shelf, peruse and return.

＊

In the woods across the road from our cottage, where I used to play, there is now Elm Lane and Birch Lane, running parallel to each other and parallel to the lake road. A few years ago, when I first started coming back here to snoop around, Elm and Birch were still dirt, but now they're paved. My forts and spots in the woods are now indistinguishable, lost in the gardens and barbecue pits. I think I could still find these places in the woods if structures weren't obscuring the landscape, but I don't trespass to test out my theory. I limit my trespassing to our old place. Elm and Birch Lanes are lined with structures on either side, owned by people who couldn't get places on the lake, or maybe couldn't afford them.

My dad used to complain about anyone who would make the grounds around a cabin look like a park. Lawns, planted flowers. Certainly that's what's happened to these woods, to Elm Lane and Birch Lane. Who needs landscaping and tulip beds when you have trilliums and wild violets?

I've brought my bike along on this nostalgia trip. I take it out now and coast down Elm Lane. I've got a mountain bike now, not a single speed Schwinn like the one I rode with my pal Joel Saari, the whole ninety miles from home up to the cottage, age fourteen. This spot off Elm Lane could be where I built a fort of fallen trees in a deer hole. This could be where my friend Al and I carried our sleeping bags to camp in the woods.

E. B. White understood what I called "the woods across the street," the imagination's need for the undeveloped, the left-alone. He admits his "camp" in Maine (we never called them that in the Midwest) was hardly the wilderness, untraversed and untrammeled. "But although it wasn't wild, it was a fairly large and undisturbed lake," he writes, "and there were places in it which, to a child at least, seemed infinitely remote and primeval." I reread his story of his return to his boyhood grounds, and think maybe we have something important in common, some question as to whether it's a place itself or the fact that we mourn its loss that best indicates its value.

When I was about twelve I said to whoever would listen, "When they start building cottages across the road, that's when I move out." As if I thought that saying it could stop the development. As if at twelve I could decide to move anywhere. My own private myth of wilderness was being violated by this layering of structures and people looking for their shot at paradise. My uncle Virgil, who himself lived year-round across the road from a lake, laughed at my pronouncement.

But he didn't tell me I was wrong. Uncle Virgil laughed at just about everything, which is what made him such a pleasant guy. "Well Carleton," he would say to my dad as the three of us strolled around the property after dinner and admired the pine trees that he had helped my dad plant. "Well Carlie old boy, should we light one up?" And Virgil would pull out a Kent and my dad a Lucky Strike, and my dad would wear that poker-faced look he had as he thought of what to say next, something that would make everybody laugh. Virgil laughed the loudest.

The smoking likely helped kill each of them years hence. But I have no interest in time travel to undo their pleasure that day, these two brothers by marriage. I can say what my interests are not more easily than what they are. Another symptom of the disease, I think. Nostalgia as malaise.

At the end of Birch Lane now I see a couple trailers, one with the light on inside, one with an old school bus rusting alongside the garage. The bus had probably been made into a camper by some hippies who later grew respectable and bought this place, their corner of the woods. "Cuddihy and East Pabst Drive" reads a mock street sign. There's a Pabst Beer sticker on the back of the old rusted-out bus. I suppose it's a nice retreat on a weekday if the neighbors aren't in. But if they're in residence you likely can smell their cigarettes and cooking oil, can hear what TV programs they like and how they bid a good hand at bridge. The people who bought this place are no longer hippies just as the vehicle is no longer a bus, but a rusted hull. Things change.

✳

I'm at the cottage with Linda, the woman who will later become my wife. We are living together and I already know her well, but this is the first time I've taken her to this place. Her two sons are here, my future stepsons, nine and eleven years old. We have driven in our tiny car the long way from our home in southern Minnesota to northern Wisconsin—too long a drive to get only to this leaking shack on this overbuilt lake, the reasons we will eventually sell the place.

The fishing is no longer good on the lake, but Linda and the boys do not know this, and the many fish they catch—stunted panfish who bite on any piece of worm dropped to the proper depth—satisfy them so totally and completely that I am satisfied. This is family life, what I heretofore had never experienced as grown man. We fish as I did when I was a child, except that my three companions seem to have much more patience than I did as a child. I have never known these domestic joys, and I feel now less like that child bent over his fire in the sand on cool nights. I'm more a part of the world, the way you're supposed to be if you're an adult.

Back at the cottage Linda fillets all the little fish so that we don't have to clean them. For her, an immigrant from Hong Kong, this preparation of the fish is just daily life, and she works quickly through the pail of bluegills and sunfish. For an American man who is a fisherman like I am, her skill at preparing and cooking fish in itself merits a marriage proposal. Victor, the older of the two boys, is a city kid, old enough to remember life in Hong Kong, and the woods and the rustic setting satisfy him less. He is reluctant to take a fish off the hook. He is grossed out by the smell and look of the old privy, so that we notice he is eating less at meals than he usually does, hoping not to have to visit the outhouse again before we leave at the end of the weekend.

Roy, the younger boy, is another matter. He continually asks, just as we're finishing one activity, "What are we going to do next?" He wears a smile permanently, dashes from boat to marsh to edge of the woods as if any or all of it might be taken from him without notice. We go out in the boat and I teach him to row, sitting behind him on the middle seat while he laughs and, together, we make choppy progress. He reminds me of what I remember of myself.

For the last days of our vacation, my mother has joined us at the cottage, this only the second or third time she's met my new family. "I've forgotten what it's like to have two boys around," she tells me, and I've forgotten that she would remember such a thing that way. By the end of the weekend she is warm in a way that I remember her seldom being, smiling at Roy's pranks and antics, trying to bring Victor out of himself a little, offering Linda help with the fish that she doesn't really need.

As we're about to leave we take pictures by the cottage back door, the grass grown long in the driveway. My mother stands behind the younger son with hands over his chest. Then Mom snaps a picture of Linda and me. And then, what are we going to do next? Roy is to take a picture of my mother and me. I can see that he's not holding the camera straight, and in the picture that results, the cottage is at a child's uncertain angle, me laughing and holding my hand up to show him to straighten the camera, trying to correct his depiction of the world.

Once more to the lake, this time with his own son, E. B. White wrote:

I began to sustain the illusion that…I was my father. This sensation persisted, kept cropping up all the time we were there. It was not an entirely new feeling, but in this setting it grew much stronger. I seemed to be living a dual existence. I would be in the middle of some simple act, I would be picking up a bait box or laying down a table fork, or would be saying something, and suddenly it would be not I but my father who was saying the words or making the gesture.

Maybe it's not the loss of the past that brings melancholy to one who merely trespasses in the present; it's the sadness that the past experience might not be repeated for the young.

What are we going to do next?

✳

"This modern stuff, you can have it," my father would say, and he said it increasingly as he got older. His pronouncements left me, as a kid, with a feeling of helplessness, as if I had missed the best of life, which took place before I was born. My dad told stories, for instance, of taking the train north out of Green Bay early in the morning, getting out at a stop somewhere in the woods. He and his sisters would spend the day picking blueberries. They had the spot to themselves. And then in the evening they'd flag down the passing train again to catch a ride home.

"But you can't stop progress," my father would end these stories, another of his bromides, delivered with the implication that although progress couldn't be stopped, it would be better if it could. He always waved his hands for emphasis as he spoke, cutting the air to make his point undeniable. "The only thing that matters now," he complained, "is the almighty buck." He would sneer slightly as he said this, except that he had something of a poker face, as I said, so that his pronouncements seemed more understated than his waving hands would let on. He used these last two expressions—"can't stop progress," and "almighty buck"—less as he got older, and I don't know if that's because their truth had become self-evident, or because he preferred not to remind himself of that truth. Whatever the reason for change, the world was going to go the way it was going to go, and the desires of one person for some peace and space were not going to be taken into account. That much was clear.

A few months before he died, when my father knew he was dying, my brother made a video tape of him talking about his life. He tells the blueberry picking story again, and ends it with another of his favorite hasty generalizations. "Now," he says of his favorite blueberry grounds along the tracks, "it's all built up. All spoiled." He draws out those last two words like someone ending a children's story, "and they lived happily ever after." "All built up. *All spoiled.*" He bounces his eyeglasses a few times against his upper leg, looks off into space. On his face is that bemused look that says he doesn't know what exactly to say next, and he knows that nothing he, or anyone, can say will be enough. Maybe this time around, the ending of the blueberry story is tempered by the knowledge of death. That he hasn't that much longer to feel the affront of needless development, the great land grab from nature. Another of his favorite lines after retirement was, "Somebody else can worry about it now." He knows that soon all worry will cease for him. But there is his disapproval just the same of the loss of freedom of place. The idea that you could go where you will in the outdoors, right at hand. I think my father understood the foolishness of human activity taken up under the guise of progress. The goal of adding to the stuff of the world to make money for oneself, nature be damned.

It's an ironic vision, one not measured to instill optimism in the next generation, of which I happened to be a member. And that's my burden. And that's why I'm back one more time, I think—to find a place in the woods to set the burden down and walk away.

✳

"We'd buy the cottage under two conditions," went a family story. "If they put a porch on the front and added a stone fireplace in the living room."

The fireplace was a grand construction for so humble a dwelling. Made with stones gathered from the area, it stood high above the green roofline, and heated at least half of the uninsulated summer cottage (a small gas stove took care of the other half.) Arriving at the cottage on spring and fall Friday evenings, we would unload the car, and I would sit on the end of the ancient couch nearest the fireplace. My dad would build a fire that would quickly throw heat. Knowing I was cold, he'd say, "It will be warm as toast here in no time." It wasn't exactly true, but the fire did have an immediate effect. He worked quickly and got good results. What I didn't know then was how much satisfaction building the fire gave him, that he wanted to do this for me.

Often we'd need a fire even in June, and we kept a wooden clothes rack next to the stones, on the side where a couple of vents sent heat into the room. On that rack wet swimming suits would hang to dry. Outside, nailed to the north side of the house was the one of our several thermometers that gave the most accurate reading. Afternoons in the shoulder seasons my brother and I would check the temperature several times an hour, willing the red mercury up toward 70 degrees, the point at which the family thought it reasonable to drive to the public beach and go in the water for a swim.

The porch and the fireplace: they were the two distinguishing features of our plain little cabin. Each was finely done in and of itself, but their being attached to the four-room cottage situated next to a swamp; their being added on after the cabin was finished—that was the rub. For this was Wisconsin, and each November when we closed the place for the winter, we couldn't close winter out. My parents would tack clear plastic over the screens on windows and doors. They'd clear the pipes, close flues, and extinguish pilots, lean logs against the screen doors that otherwise might blow open in the winter wind. But the frost would have its way with the place, set as it was not on a basement or a slab, but on construction blocks under each corner. Set on the lowest point on the lake, the building was heaved and pitched all winter as if it were on a great sea. The porch had a flat roof that held a season's worth of snow, and it stood on its own two blocks; the fireplace was many times heavier than the house and rested on a concrete slab. So while the house might move one direction, the porch and fireplace would lean their own ways. Each winter the house did this modern dance, its lines and angles shifting. In spring, the place leaked.

And the monolith fireplace, over time, sank into the ground beneath it. Leaned away, like a drunk taking years to pass out flat on his back. Those side vents that in early years dried out wet swimwear, eventually fed their warmth half in and half out of the house. The gun rack above the mantle had to come down, the civil war era rifle hanging a good twenty degrees off plumb. Then the vase on the mantle also leaned askew, so we thought it would slide off and crash to the floor. Through the crack between the fireplace and the wall, mice and squirrels came in for winter residence. We stuffed insulation around the chimney, more each year. In college when my pals and I came up for a January trip, even after we'd had a roaring blaze for hours, frost would remain like a white day's growth of beard on the stones facing inside.

Eventually, after my college years, when I saw the place less, my parents had a local crew knock the fireplace down. They built some thin paneling where it had stood. Hung a few blown-up hunting snapshots. They said someday they'd put in a Franklin stove. They never did.

*

Asked for years what his ideas were about how to fix the cottage, my father finally began to answer, with that bemused expression of his, "To hell with it, let it go." That always got a good laugh at the extended family cocktail party. And it finally seemed the best solution from a man who had maybe come to terms with his limitations. Dad was retired by then, and maybe had come to accept the time he had left. Prioritizing. Not caring about that which he was not meant to care. He lit his pipe. He drank a beer. We changed the subject.

For years he had wheelbarrowed that sand down to the shore to make a beach for his kids to swim, so we wouldn't have to drive to the public swimming beach whenever that thermometer had been willed up to 70 degrees. But the sand never took; the beach was never to be. And in retirement, a time in life that earlier he had imagined living all summer and fall at the cottage, he found surprisingly that he cared less about the place. The reason, I think, was that his sons had grown and gone.

About ten years after my father died we sold the cottage. Got much less for it than we should have, the boom in "vacation property" (that phrase did not exist in my boyhood) just getting off the ground. The previous ten years we had found less and less reason to go there. My family and I lived far away from the place and didn't like the long drive in that little car we had. And then at some point I realized that even though my childhood had played out there, that the cottage was and had always been my father's place.

My father believed something about the land that I also now believe, that the land has an inherent worth and even goodness apart from human endeavor. I think now that this shared belief also helped us to love him. Is this nostalgia too?

"Ah, the cottage!" my mother said twenty years after my father was gone, about the time we were selling her house and moving her into a nursing home, her mind going, the past going away once and for all. "The cottage— those were the good years."

I don't know why I was so surprised to hear her say that, since it was so obviously true. Perhaps because, like many Midwestern families, mine never dwelt on the emotional life. Perhaps because I did not want to be reminded myself that those times (and that place) could never return. While I myself evidenced the symptoms, I did not like hearing that others also suffered from the disease. I somehow wanted to tell my parents always that things weren't so bad, to reassure as one might reassure children, and thereby reassure myself.

Incurable. Nostalgia is not a state of mind that passes like a 48-hour bug. It's a condition to live with, like high blood pressure or allergies. Like having one leg shorter than the other (my father had that) or being too quick-tempered for your own good (I have that), or prone to exaggeration of argument or story—like this story.

We may not want to live in the other, sober world. Maybe E. B. White knew that too, and knew that one response was to bear witness and then go on. I've been reading it wrong all these years. It's not once more *to the lake*, but *once more* to the lake. *Once* more. If all moments collapse to one, there truly is no reason to go back. Not that that is satisfying. Not that we don't want most what we can never have.

ON HEARING/ON LISTENING ⸻

A T 65, I'M USUALLY THE YOUNGEST IN THE BAND. WE PLAY THE OLD-est of old standards—very little from after the War, plus novelty tunes, blues. The most senior player is a trumpeter who, even if you ask him, won't give his age. I don't ask.

The trumpet is a very physical instrument, and Stan confessed to me once that he never practiced. The band leader introduces him as having "that fat New Orleans sound," which, I thought, is likely a result of him being as old as he is, and never practicing on the most unforgiving of horns. It all depends on what you mean by fat.

Stan is a sweet man. His wife comes to the gig sometimes and sits at a front table, and she is also sweet, which may be one reason Stan is so sweet. The turn in this story comes when I tell you that Stan is also a good musi-cian. He seldom looks at a chart, always offers me his chart if the leader calls a tune I don't know. Stan doesn't need to look at the music. Stan can hear everything.

Except Stan can no longer hear very well. That's the second turn in this story. In our pleasant conversations on breaks, I can see Stan's eyes read-ing my lips. Sometimes his responses to me are non sequiturs that seem to change the subject. We're talking about a player he likes, then we're talking about a good movie he just saw. Sometimes he speaks so quietly himself that I can't really hear him either. He wears a hearing aid in each ear, but these little machines are notoriously ineffective when the background noise is as thick as it usually is in a lively bar when the band is on break.

The band itself doesn't play loud. Sound on "stage" (actually a cramped space near the front window so the owner can fill as many tables as possible.

Sometimes the bell of my saxophone seems to disturb the closest diner's primavera) is reasonably clear. Most of the time Stan does fine. And when Stan hits the right notes, the bluest notes, the audience loves him. Like most audiences, of course, they listen with their eyes. Their eyes hear only this round and sweet man of indeterminate age, seated behind his trumpet as if it's an extra, somewhat awkward appendage. They can see he is having a good time. And thus, so are they. *Miss, what's the special tonight?*

One time, on a simple blues, Stan is playing his solo, the bell of the horn in the air, angled over his unneeded music stand, as if he's emptying the last of a sweet liquid into his mouth. He has that fat sound; the notes splotch and settle on pitch. Problem is, those right notes fall clearly into a key other than the one in which the rest of the band is playing. The bass player, who like Stan has an ear that I admire, looks puzzled for a bar or two, then catches my eye and we both smile. Now the guitar player hears, and the singer. Stan plays on. Every note a good note, a right note, if only the rest of the band were wrong.

The audience watches on, chats on, eats and drinks and, not knowing how to listen, doesn't hear. The musicians are listening, but must pretend they're not. And after all, it was always that kind of gig, where all of us in the band could drink a few beers, have fun, but still do pretty well when we counted up the tip jar around one a.m. Stan plays resoundingly, falling off the curb on a few notes, as the trumpet would have it, but I'm not sure anyone in the crowd notices that either.

Then after Stan's chorus, the singer comes in, spot on in the key we thought we'd all agreed to.

The next turn in this story comes when I never again hear Stan play an entire chorus in the wrong key. Not that night, or any night thereafter.

A few months later, the leader of the band, ten years older than me and ten years younger than Stan I would guess, says that playing this gig once a month has become stressful, and he needs a break. A few months later, it's apparent the break is to be permanent. I never see or hear Stan again. The bandleader says they held a birthday party for him recently and the cake gave away his secret: Happy 90th, Stan.

I wasn't at the party, but I heard everyone played just fine.

I know Stan always listened. What I'll go to my grave dying to know is, when Stan played that chorus in the wrong key, what did the rest of the band sound like to him? What did he sound like to himself? And what did the two have in common? What notes did they share?

✳

The bass player I usually work with, in another band, also plays with one of the better jazz big bands in our city. There are many of these bands around. They're comprised mostly of band directors, mostly male, all good players who miss performing and take rehearsal as their night out away from job and family.

Greg asked if I could sub in the jazz tenor sax chair in his band at a rehearsal the following evening. Big bands are to the small group jazz that I have been playing forever, what professional football is to modern dance. Both involve heightened physical activity, and that's about the end of the similarities.

OK, I exaggerate—because I'm so good at it. But big bands, with their screaming trumpets and driving drum set, their outrageous displays of technique, seem to me like the masculine side of jazz. More body than soul. Sure, big bands can play a ballad, but it usually features a flugelhorn or alto saxophone playing sixteen bars of a melody that's reminiscent of something you've heard in a TV show theme. The arrangement will feature flute and muted trumpet backgrounds. In the concert program, the ballad will serve as a breather between two charts featuring garish dynamics and passages in which fifteen people play together a line of music that no one of them individually would take the trouble to learn. There's musicianship, and teamwork, to be sure. But big bands were never my thing.

So I warned Greg: I last played in a big band … (pause to calculate) thirty-one years ago.

"That's OK," he said. "I think you'll have fun."

To be sure, I ended up laughing a lot during the two-hour rehearsal—like whenever I didn't have the horn in my mouth. But I was laughing at myself. How the years had played yet another trick on me. You see, I had forgotten how to read music.

The scrawl of notes on the charts put before me, some of which draped over either side of my music stand, suggested to me the Chinese calligraphy that my wife practices at home in her spare time. Except it was as if someone had taken a damp cloth and lightly blurred the ink with a swipe of the hand. I tried on my music reading glasses. I tried my regular bifocals. I tried no glasses at all. No difference. I couldn't tell the forest for the trees, which stubbornly held all of their leaves through the long winter of the rehearsal.

I don't mean to say I can't read music at all. My bandmates in our quartet will often put a chart before me with a melody and chord changes written out. But unless we have a guest on trumpet or flute or more, I'm the only one playing that melody line. The notes are more like suggestions, like getting a letter from a parent, filled with good advice. I play what I want and make it fit.

The big band's players tonight are sight reading some of these tunes (meaning they're seeing the music for the first time) just like me. "There are a variety of reading levels in the band, so you don't have to worry about not being able to keep up," Greg had said. But these musicians, even the least of them, are archaeologists and linguists. The hieroglyphics on the page, with their dotted eighth and sixteenth patterns, their manic accidentals, are all in a day's work for them. The signs and codas will send me back to page one as they should, but several beats behind the rest of the band.

I'm smiling, I'm laughing at myself, at lessons learned. I used to be able to sight read—the secret of which to is to read ahead, to be able to play a bar of music with your hands while your eyes and brain are already looking several bars ahead. In only thirty brief years, that knack had mysteriously disappeared.

"What's the tempo on this chart?" the band leader asks from the lead alto chair. "I have written down 135," the drummer replies. "That's here," says the leader. "A one, two, a one two three four..." and they're off, and once left by the side of the road, I can only laugh again.

But my first rule is do no harm. I figure out eventually that if I play the beginning of a difficult phrase, and then move my fingers in time for a bit, and play the end of the phrase with the rest of the sax section, it sounds to those not seated close to me that I know what I'm doing.

I hadn't realized how much of an ear player I'd become, how much I've come to depend on listening. Listening better, hearing more, is a skill I'd worked toward. Tonight, I found myself listening to what the other saxes were playing on a fast passage, and then since most patterns repeat themselves, I would just memorize the sounds and play them along with the others when those notes next appeared on the page. With this, and being able to play the easy passages, I was playing maybe sixty percent of the ink on the page. And to the trumpets, trombones, and rhythm section, paying attention to their own business, it probably sounded like I was getting things right ninety percent of the time.

"When in doubt, lay out," my college big band director used to say. That is, don't make a mistake and play when no one else is playing, something the back row of seats in the auditorium will hear. Such good advice.

Opposed to this is the directive of improvised jazz, which is to make it up as you go along. Trust the fates. Never know the end of a musical sentence until after you begin writing it. Made things will have the unity you bring to them. Worry later about coherence, and "later" never comes, so don't worry at all.

How to know on which occasions to lay out till you're sure, and when to just wing it and play?

How much this is like the lives we all lead outside the rehearsal room. Musicians or not, we each listen to the moments as we live them. Play or wait, play or rest. Each directive, each impulse conflicts with its opposing number, intertwines with its opposite to make a world.

✳

Beethoven was near the end of his life, but still doing what he could to keep people from knowing about his deafness, which by this point was profound. He was conducting an orchestra in rehearsal of one of his works—let's say it was the Ninth Symphony, since that makes the best story.

In this story, Beethoven, knowing his score by heart, conducted with his eyes closed. Or perhaps he'd just finished writing the movement the orchestra was rehearsing, and his eyes were buried in the score. Choose the detail you like best; this was all a long time ago.

Then for some reason the orchestra and chorus (Was it the last movement of the Ninth? Were there singers present too?) all stopped at once. Perhaps the manager of the theater walked in, waving his hands, to announce what time the green room would be available before next weekend's opening night. Did the nineteenth century Vienna concert halls have green rooms? If so, were the green rooms green?

Or maybe the concert hall was old and heavy snow had fallen over Vienna all that winter. And now, finally, the roof began to leak, and pieces of plaster from the ceiling were dropping like light rain over the music stands of the second violins. Stop!

Or maybe a malcontent rushed into the empty theater and shouted fire.

What happened next, though, was that the eyes of the orchestra's players rose up from their parts to the figure of Beethoven—who continued to conduct with as much passion, as much vigor as he'd had the moment before. His shock of hair, unkempt now, thrown from side to side, a half second behind the beat. The great eyes indeed closed, as if alive in death, as if dying but still in this life.

He listened through his dark silence, and for him the music went on, glorious and undiminished.

❋

After a week of a high dose of anabolic steroids, I'm having my hearing tested for a second time. The steroids, I was warned, might bring about strange side effects, but mostly they made everything more wonderful than it should have been: great workouts at the Y, walks that exhausted my small dog, a sharp appetite at every meal, a desire to clean and organize every drawer and file in my home office. Good practice on the horn. The hope was, the ENT specialist told me, that if my hearing loss was recent and sudden, sometimes the steroids can undo what's been done, and some of the hearing would return.

Part of me, most of me, knew that this was not to transpire. I started noticing a couple years back in my classes that young people—the college students I taught—simply didn't talk as loud as they used to (I still think this is true—something to do with having learned tolerance so well that one's ideas need not be broadcast at high volume.) Even before that, I'd noticed difficulty hearing in those fashionable restaurants with the high ceilings, uncarpeted floors, open kitchen, and loud not-background music. I'd end up reading lips of even the person directly across from me. Anyone on my periphery or farther away might as well have been seated in a Mack Sennett movie.

I'm seated now in a soundproof booth, as if in a 1950s quiz show. I'm fitted with a set of heavy headphones, very Walter Cronkite, if you remember that. The test begins with beeping sounds in my "good" or right ear. They are different pitches and volumes, like a busy signal on an old land line telephone. Press the button when you hear the tone, is the technician's simple instruction. I feel myself guessing, but figure I'm guessing right much of the time. A lot is at stake, trying to find out the truth, so I'm listening as closely as I can.

Now to the "bad" or left ear. Same story. I'm acing this test, I think to myself. Repeat these words after me: house... house...color...color. "Simple," I'm smiling inside.

But the result is exactly the same as it had been the week before: in the bad ear, some loss at the highest pitches, which is normal. But significant loss in the mid-range, which is not.

"But I heard the beeps begin and end," I protest, "and at the right times, too. I repeated every word right back to you"

"Yes," says the tech, "You heard the beeps at the right time, but in order for you to hear them, I had to jack up the volume."

*

As a college freshman, I had to get up five mornings a week and trudge through campus and over a river to make it to music theory class at eight a.m. Not easy.

The teacher seemed impossibly old to us—even older than I am now, it occurs to me as I write. But everyone liked and respected him, so we made it to class. In fact, upon his retirement, the Music Department named the concert hall after him.

During Wisconsin winters, this trek was especially foreboding—those mornings below zero when crossing the bridge over the Chippewa River, you could swear that you were hearing cold. Some combination of ice sheets cracking and popping over the moving water below, and the indefinite pitch of boots taking their paces on the snow-covered walkway. But even on the coldest winter evenings, after the workday, we would see Professor Gantner, the old music theoretician, walking home wearing only a tweed sport coat and wool scarf. Word was he was part Eskimo, but even then I didn't believe it.

One morning in class something happened that caught my attention, woke me up. Mr. Gantner was talking about dissonance, the sound of a chord that grates at the ear, a sound that sets out to displease or provoke.

"Now," he said, seated at the piano, "ideas of what dissonance is change over time. The music doesn't change; the listeners change."

(OK, so what, thought the eighteen-year-old minds in the room.)

"Take for instance, this chord."

Then he played what to all of us students was a perfectly interesting and beautiful arrangement of notes.

"To my ear, that's harsh."

He made a slightly unpleasant face, which I imagine was hard for him.

"Can you hear it? Eww…"

He pounded the chord harder, repeatedly. Then the face grew calm.

"But I know to you young people, its sounds perfectly fine."

He was right again.

It's entirely too romantic, entirely too good of a story, for me to contend, as I'd like to, that that moment may be the first time I truly listened, listened that carefully. I could hear the chord as pleasant, and I thought I could hear it the way he did as well.

Not all situations allow themselves to be resolved so pleasantly. I remember equally well a concert hall, about seven years later, where I'm sitting in a master class with the saxophonist Dexter Gordon, one of my musical heroes. Dexter was at the top of his form in those years, having returned from a self-imposed European exile back to the States, where he won Downbeat polls and had several albums that were topping the jazz charts. His status as a celebrity, which was burnished a few years later with his Oscar-nominated performance for best actor in *Round Midnight*, was taking shape.

After some great playing with his band, it was time for Dexter to take some questions from the assembled students. But Dexter was a man of few words. Few words, but words often cast in poetic diction. He talked slowly, deliberately, with a warm yet booming, low voice. Like so many great musicians, he talked the way he played.

Most of the questions were, of course, idiotic:

"What do you think of Michael Jackson?" Like Dexter, he too was at the top of his game just then.

Dexter paused. "I think he's a very good," and then another pause, "... dancer."

It was politic. And then an even more revealing exchange.

"What do you think of the younger sax players who've come to the fore in recent years?"

The usual pause, and then.

"I haven't ... heard them."

Everyone was too polite to press the issue, to break his diplomatic silence. But all these years later, I think it may have been an honest answer. Of course he knew who those young players were. He had to have heard the best of them, at least in passing.

And while their playing, to him or anyone, was hardly dissonant, Dexter perhaps could not hear them the way we heard them, the way they heard themselves. And he knew it, so that's what he said.

✳

I'm playing an office Christmas party. But not just any office. This is the big downtown law firm where Larry, my piano player, works as director of pro bono services. The party is informal; not all of the people are wearing dark business suits. What's more, it looks like the party started an hour or more before the band arrived, given the good cheer that's in everyone's hands and, one assumes, their tanks. Larry's wife is sitting in with us on a few tunes, on flute. And she started accordion lessons a few months ago, and brought that axe as well (Accordion! Really?) That's just how relaxed this gig is. Drink up, season's greetings, and joy to the world for the rest of the afternoon at least.

Or so I thought. Larry and I have been blowing down our holiday set list—tunes which Larry has rearranged to sound like they were all written by Pontius Pilate. It's our preference, our brand, if you will. "Silent Night," "Angels We Have Heard on High," "I'll Be Home for Christmas"—all redone in a minor key, and/or cast into 5/4 or 7/4 time. It's Christmas with the drapes closed to keep out that annoying winter sunlight. The light of the world here is running on worn batteries.

Then the word comes from the woman facilitating the event that someone has complained: "Tell the damn band to play something up tempo and in a major key." Is this someone high up on the food chain of the firm? Like maybe one of those seven-figure partners? Some of whom dislike Larry because, as pro bono director, he contributes no billable hours and actually decides how best to cost the firm money? Oh yes, indeed it is, the facilitator tells us.

It's so stereotypically "lawyer" that I wonder for a minute if we've been written into a TV series. Not only to throw his weight around and tell the band to liven it up—even though everyone in the crowded, noisy, happy room seems to be having a good time at the firm's considerable expense. But also to let the world know that he can hear the difference between major and minor, between common time and everything else, and that his internal metronome can approximate 100 beats per minute. "Your witness," he might as well add, and "oh by the way, fuck you."

Larry and I scan though the set list we've prepared. Not one tune is in a major key! Now that is extreme. Quick pull something up. No prob, let's do our Bill Evans version of "Alice in Wonderland," which Larry counts out a good twenty beats per minute faster than either Bill or we have ever done it.

Then the answer to every live musician's dilemma: We take a break. We fill our plates from the gorgeous spread—crab dip and decorated cookies, fresh veg, shrimp the size of Baja California. Before we go back up to play, we inquire, has Scrooge left the building? Oh yes, indeed, he has. He's made his point, shown what he can hear when he listens. We can go back to our minor obsession.

Because to us, what we hear in those minor modes—the Dorian, the Aeolian—is so much richer, so much more fulfilling than their major cousins. Besides, by mid-December hasn't everyone had enough of the happy happy jolly jolly Xmas Benzedrine designed to get you to max out your credit card before blowing your brains out by year's end?

Minor is to major as Bogart is to Donnie Osmond. As the James Cagney of *Public Enemy* is to the James Cagney of *I'm a Yankee Doodle Dandy*. Minor is to major what midnight is away from light-polluted sky over the parking lot of IKEA on Black Friday. Major is sugar. Minor is cream.

At this darkest time of the year, and in this year of Trump, of unmitigated climate change—a year that seems the darkest in memory—let the sound of the dark fill our souls until we remember why we're alive.

✳

In the weeks' that follow my diagnosis, "Sensorineural hearing loss, moderate," I imagine the worst. There aren't too many deaf musicians around. But equally true, I'm not Beethoven and for the world at large my loss is not theirs. Even Stan played in the right key every time but one.

So I go back to playing my saxophone, telling Linda I can't hear her when the water's running, and trying to identify the pitch of the tinnitus in my left ear. Something around a concert e-flat.

"The kind of hearing loss you have, where you can't hear in restaurants and loud places, hearing aids really don't do a lot of good," the doctor told me. Nice to know. I guess.

The doc's answer to all my questions is the same. Will this get worse, and when? Will it spread to another ear? What's the cause? What recourse?

We don't know.

As in, the only way you can know the future now is if you have no future at all.

✳

Linda and I will be in Stratford-upon-Avon one night only, and I'm determined to see a play. I go to book the tickets months in advance, and find it's *Troilus and Cressida* or nothing. One of Shakespeare's "problem plays." I'm no scholar and wonder if that appellation means simply that no one is sure of what the Bard thought he was doing in writing them. I have problems with anything based on the Trojan War because I can never remember which guys are Greeks and which guys are Trojans.

But we may never get back to England. I buy the tickets.

I try to prepare by reading the text of *T&C*, but can't wade through it—it's a problem, all right. So we find a filmed BBC production from the 70s and we screen it on consecutive nights with dinner for our edification. I say consecutive nights because the thing is so slow that we can only do one act per night. In a week, curtain.

We're in our seats now, our one-night-only, eight rows back, beautiful theater experience. We've had an extra cup of tea, determined to stay awake the whole three and half hours. It's Shakespeare. This is Stratford. It's a matter of should.

But then we find no such regimen is necessary: the production is magnificent. It can be funny and wise and cold and hard in adjacent moments. Turns out that that may have been Shakespeare's point. The costuming can have Troilus in one scene dressed as a stereotypical Trojan with a sword and one of those plumed helmets. But then some of the characters wear side arms that would make an NRA member smile. And then when Hector's body is dragged through the battleground, it's done from the rear of Achilles' real live-onstage motorcycle. There are a lot of tattoos and black leather. Hell's Angels circa 1150 AD. This is maybe the greatest theater I've ever seen.

And then there's the music, live music. It's the element that even in advance I was most intrigued by. It's entirely percussion. Troilus is a war play, remember, and the thunder of battle, and the crash and burn of human ego and desire is well represented. Gongs, chimes, bells, vibes, snare drums, bass drums, and then dozens of percussive instruments, the sounds of which are new to most human ears. The composer, Evelyn Glennie, is the world's most famous percussionist, the program tells us. She even does solo percussion concerts.

Incidentally, and only incidentally, she has been profoundly deaf since age 12. She learned to hear, to listen, using other parts of her body. I'm not sure what that entails, but I'm sure that I like the idea. Given the difficulty most people have listening even with their ears, I'm in awe at the prospect and the process of listening with one's hands and feet. Given the music I'm hearing tonight, the composer has taught herself to listen closely and well.

Only one element of the production had me wondering. In the play, Cassandra, as in myth, is the mad sister of Hector and Troilus. Like most mad people in old literature, she can, of course, prophesize the future. She can foresee the violent end of her brother Hector, but then as always in these stories, her prophecy is dismissed. She's simply hysterical, right?

To my eye and ear, there was something different about the performance of the actor playing Cassandra, but I couldn't say just what. A tall woman dressed in what seemed typical Tom-o-Bedlam garb, she would gesticulate wildly, darting ungracefully about the stage. Sudden screams. Guttural sounds. Another character would interpret her sounds and gestures for King Priam's onlooking family.

It was only later that I learned that the actor playing Cassandra so broadly was actually signing Casandra's lines as Shakespeare wrote them. She's the first deaf actor ever cast by the Royal Shakespeare Company.

It's telling that in some later versions of this story, Cassandra has been blessed and cursed with her gift for prophesy by snakes that licked and whispered in her ears. Perhaps she could not see, but hear what was to come.

＊

My dog Zachy is partly deaf, like me. He's 14, which is 72 in Bichon years, a website tells me. We're the oldest of buddies and our lives run in these pleasing parallels, if at a slower pace than ten years before: I can't make out the dialogue on television if Linda is in the same room rattling the pages of the schoolwork she's grading; Zachy the dog can't hear me coming down the hall if his head is turned the other way. Sometimes I turn up the volume on the TV; sometimes Zachy nearly gets stepped on for failure to scurry out of the way.

It was maybe five years ago that I was hurrying my drive home from work because I knew a cut from my band's new CD was going to be spun on the local jazz station. I'd been gone for several days, and when I came in the door, Zachy was excited to see me and not aware the reason for my haste was something other than being anxious to see him. I petted him quickly and sat back in a chair next to the radio in the dining room. Zachy jumped in my lap and settled in for a nap with his head on my thigh, content. The jazz station was in the middle of a public service announcement, yadda yadda yadda.

I didn't know what cut from our CD they'd play. But then it started. We did "Night and Day" by Cole Porter with a Latin beat. On live dates, the tune would start always with an unaccompanied improvised solo by me; for the CD, I wanted to keep it tight and not take up disk space. So I skipped the solo and just started with the unaccompanied melody. Those first notes, two eighths and a dotted half on concert G: "Night and Day," … and then, "you are the one…."

Zachy is a companion dog and chief among the pursuits of his day are eating, sleeping, and seeing what I'm up to in various parts of the house. He will venture down to my basement practice studio, nudge open the door with his little nose, and see and hear me making that sound on the big yellow saxophone. It must seem very loud to him, and I suppose rather pointless. He may be right about the pointless part. So when he's sure I'm not up to anything important, he will about-face and scoot up the stairs.

That's backstory. In this moment I'm telling you about, I'm in the antique dining room chair, beer opened, shoes off, dog on my lap. The DJ cues us up and talks us in.

Those first three notes: *night and day*…. And then the little miracle. Zachy's head pops upright from his deep repose. His posture at the ready, his attention wrapped around the moving elements. That concert g on the tenor saxophone….

He recognized it. He knew the sound of his master's voice, coming through that golden tube, that useless contraption with the conical bore, producing that music we all are made of. Loving me as a good dog must, he couldn't help but listen. The tones were packed away in the part of the brain reserved for familiar sound. And in the next moment or two, I knew they would always be there, without regard to dynamics or tone color, volume or pitch. The ineffable, internalized sound of coming home. Or the sound of waiting, maybe not so patiently, of knowing everything, any time of night or day, would be just all right. Knowing without sound, without saying or being told, you are the one.

THE WORLD AWAY ====

...n OR ARE WE TEMPTED TO SING PRAISES OF THE BEAUTY OF POR-
tages, like the long one along the Basswood River called The
Horse Portage. According to our outfitter, before the Boundary
Waters and Quetico were the large wilderness parks they are today, loggers
did indeed use horses to haul equipment on this mile-and-a-quarter-long
trail. You feel like a horse—or a Spartan slave—doing the horse portage.
And if, like us, you're not hefty enough to carry both a pack and a canoe
in the same trip, you cross each portage three times, there and back and
there again. So a mile-and-a-quarter portage like this one becomes nearly
a four-mile walk, two thirds of it under the weight of what you foolishly
thought you had to bring on your canoe trip. I start such portages feeling
fresh and confident; finish them feeling thirsty, sore, and overmatched. It
always seems to be raining on a portage. Or it has rained and the trail is slick
rock and deep puddles.

Being young or in outstanding physical condition should not be allowed
in this wilderness. Those who fit that description can never know how good
a cold swim feels in the evening after such work that you're not in shape for.
They can't know the numbing taste of the first sip of rum at night, or how
much more silent silence is when you've been humbled by your middle-aged
body. Consider the different varieties of silence this far back in the woods:
the water caught in your ears after a cold swim, the sky when you're the first
one out of the tent in the morning, the bits of time between cries of loons
on opposite ends of the lake. And those times on the water or around a late
fire when no one talks because no one needs to talk. There is so much sacred
here that it's hard to keep a list short enough to read.

Portaging should also keep you from being too proud. Too ambitious. Keep you from thinking that trees and water forty miles in look a lot different from trees and water twenty miles in. They're different, but are they different enough to be worth all the misery? Linda ventured with me and my pal Schmidty and his wife to the Quetico on a brief summer trip one year. Linda found the setting as beautiful as I did, but wondered—with one lake seemingly as good as the next—why we bothered to portage at all. It's a fair question.

The answer may be that we're all on some kind of portage, in the Quetico and beyond. This is an idea so corny, so obviously symbolic as to almost have to be true. We all schlep things: packs, the food we need to eat, the shelter we need to stay out of the rain. We also bear crosses. In between the varied experiences of our excursions, the scenery we see going by in life, there has to be this drudgery that turns muscles and tendons to salty twine. Drudgery looking at its own feet. I have all the character I need, thanks, and this won't build any more.

We're always walking between two lakes: the known lake of the present and the unknown lake that's next and which is always more beautiful because you haven't seen it yet. That is the world away from the known world, the next world that awaits.

Only in life, we don't know what portage we're on, do we? Doubt is natural, meaning it's part of nature, stupid. From the canoe, we look for and find the lowest spot in the treeline that marks the beginning of the portage trail. We pull up to a beach or rocky inlet. Maybe a stream or marsh is off to one side, flowing or draining from this lake to the next. We unstrap our gear from the boats and pile it off the trailhead, in case someone else should traverse by in the other direction. We wouldn't want to obstruct or delay the other party's leaving us alone. We strap the packs on our backs, grab paddles, life preservers (excuse me, I date myself: "personal flotation devices"), and set off.

There's usually just one path, so we simply get out of the boat and start our routine. We might begin to count our steps, and could be forgiven for that. We don't know how long before we can set all this stuff down and just look at the trees. Someone else, many people have made this trail, this trial. Maybe a parent with a child, or maybe the whole of human history, but probably nothing that dramatic. We just trust that finally we'll find ourselves on another lake.

My childhood, as I choose to remember it, was spent in the outdoors, and it resides happily there now. The lost promise that was made to me and to all North Americans was made in the outdoors—what Nick Carraway in *The Great Gatsby* called the "fresh, green breast of the new world." If we can set aside Fitzgerald's biased coloring of landscape as female inviolate, we're left with the idea that there is something that precedes humanity and is far greater than what humans are and what humans do, even though we don't know exactly what that something is.

Schmidty is having a smoke and taking a few casts at the shore once we've set up camp, and I join him down there for a respite. He says the minute before I came down the path, a family of ducks came out of the water, the mother and the line of ducklings heading off into the woods. Where the hell were they going, he wonders.

"Maybe," I say, "they were just trying to get away from you."

"Maybe," he answers, and then a pause like a sigh. We stare at the water and the air. Tree pollen is floating all directions in the breeze, the trees backlit by long sun.

"Sometimes I think of all this beauty here and how ninety-five percent of the time, there's no one here to see it," Schmidty says.

"Exactly as it should be," I answer.

Trout Fishing: A Manifesto ═══

> "Fishermen also think of the river as having
> been made with them partly in mind."
> —NORMAN McLEAN,
> *A River Runs Through It*

D RIVING OVER THE BRIDGE, HE ALWAYS SLOWS TO CHECK THE LEVEL *of the stream—even when he is not stopping to fish. No one is around today, and that's good.*

September: The cooler days have made the water high. He walks downstream to check a camping spot his brother told him about. There's a field, a fire ring with grass grown high inside. A sign, "NO CAMPING," has been turned around to face the tree it's nailed to. Does that mean no camping, or that there used to be no camping? Anyway, no one is here.

He sits down on the ground to eat his lunch, his legs stretched in front of him. In the grass, autumn wildflowers are growing, names of which he can never learn. A knee-high maple is putting on its show of red. He leans back to lie down, looks up at pieces of the sky through birch, pine, and aspen. A pair of osprey circle, following the path of the stream. How do they know where it is? He spots a third—the young.

He remembers the time he got up from a campsite, headed down to the stream in early morning, and saw first thing a scarlet tanager, the only time he's ever seen that bird. The red of its body surprised him so as to be almost painful. Its black wings were the exception that made its red the rule. He remembers the bird now for a much longer time than he had actually seen it in the first place.

This driving and walking and sitting in a field has happened many times.

❋

Getting There

The Interstate belongs to everyone and to no one. But when I turn off to a smaller road, my mood changes much as the scenery does—becoming warmer, more given to the random placement of people and objects within the frame of my windshield.

I've been driving in Wisconsin for an hour's worth of Interstate miles, but when I turn north on Highway 40, I'm home to a Wisconsin that's the May before June. The trunks of maple trees have been darkened by last night's storm. There's the new green I think I see, as if someone chose to paint it there.

The road winds up through a pass of trees, curves to reveal a pine nursery on the right, a couple of farmhouses for sale. A county cop pulls out of the state recreation area; red wing blackbirds loiter near a pond at the side of the road. An earlier stop at a McDonald's—always a bad idea—is burning up my pipes, but I was in such a hurry to get *here* and away from *there* that I did the drive-through. Now I reach for an apple to try to fill the churning emptiness inside. Soda crackers and an antacid tablet follow.

But it feels good to be moving. Someone chips up to the green on number five of the White Tail Golf and Supper Club. He's wearing white pants and a lavender shirt that billows in the breeze, and his shot is rolling toward the pin and may prove to have been a good shot, though I won't be here when the ball stops rolling (none of us will be here when the ball stops rolling.) I know he doesn't notice my car going by: he kept his head down—good form.

❋

What To Wear

I wear the same clothes every time trout fishing. Most important are a pair of old tennis shoes, since I know my feet will get wet when I walk into the water after a snag, or sometimes stand in the water to fish, or walk upstream if the way along the bank is too thick and brambly. I don't like the weight and cold discomfort of waders, and this stream isn't deep enough for the trouble. My old sneakers are more like holes with pieces of shoe around them. They're not athletic shoes.

Over a flannel shirt, on cool mornings or evenings, especially in May or September, I'll wear my light gray windbreaker. It's fifteen years old, and Linda tried to give it to the thrift shop without telling me. I liked that because it seemed like something a wife would do in a situation comedy. I like it when life imitates trashy art. I fished the jacket out of the rummage bag in the garage.

My fishing hat—formless and round—is white. It's not as old as the gray windbreaker, but it's something I found at the shore of a lake and since there was nobody around, I kept it.

After a weekend of trout fishing, having sprayed insect dope under the brim and all around the outside, I'll throw the hat in the washing machine. Some people say washing your fishing hat is bad luck. Most days, though, in this spot, I can catch trout, even when the hat is clean.

※

Getting There

I passed a bar not terribly far back that's painted purple on the west end, and yellow and green on the east. Inside, I've always imagined, a fifty-yard line runs from wall to wall up the bar—*Vikings/Packers*—the beer the same price either side of the divide. The bar is in that small part of Wisconsin that looks to the Twin Cities for its identity—bedroom communities, exurbs, places people go to get away from other people like themselves. Like everything we do, it's self-fulfilling doom as sure as other people will follow. There's a part of the American let's-move-west myth that they didn't tell us about in grade school, that there's only so much room to grow, and given the amount of room it takes to be an American, we're a doomed species. "Don't worry," a wire story says about projections of half a billion Americans by the year 2050. "We'll still only have the population density of Germany." It's reassuring till you imagine Americans living like Europeans—all in apartments or row houses, or in their old-world cities with narrow streets and no parking, so close you can hear the neighbors' arguments. And worse, they can hear yours.

Few days go by when I don't think about it—the closing down of America, the national failure to recognize the connection between open space and individual agency. I can't label my state of mind worry, since the loss is all but inevitable, this great national land grab that is endless growth. My state of mind is akin to looking away from a dead body, but knowing it's there, and what to be done?

*

The Natural Superiority of Trout Fishing

Trout Fishing is best carried out alone. On a small stream it's inconvenient to fish with someone else. One fisherman can go upstream and one down, but the problem is that usually one way yields better fishing than the other, and often both fishermen know that. So there's a chance that in a moment of selflessness or good manners, you might volunteer to go the wrong way, leaving the better fishing to your partner, and we know he doesn't deserve it.

Another problem with the one up/one down arrangement is that you have to agree before you set out what time you will meet back at the car. It might be a beautiful day, or the fish may be biting hard, but if it's quarter after six, and you said you'd be back at five-thirty and you're a half-hour tramp from the car, you're already in trouble. But are you going to walk away from a hot streak just because you said you'd meet your partner at the car at five-thirty? You might consider just not going back at all, but for that decision, too, there is hell to pay.

Conversely, if it starts raining at three-thirty—raining hard, and you agreed to meet your partner back at the car at quarter after six, well, you've got a lot of misery ahead of you, especially if you don't have a car key. Especially if the fish aren't biting.

> "Nick did not like to fish with other men
> on the river. Unless they were part of
> your party, they spoiled it."
> —ERNEST HEMINGWAY,
> *Big Two-Hearted River: Part II*

✳

Getting There

Another house for sale. I crunch a bite from my apple, finish the soda crackers and wash it down with a swig of milk. The road winds up. Junction County Trunk B. Friends from out of state are amused that Wisconsin labels its small roads by letter and not by number. I grew up with that and am amused by their amusement. It was one of those marks of becoming worldly when I found that other places didn't do it our way, but called a small road "County 210" or whatever. Perhaps the original thinking in Wisconsin was that there was no reason for any county to maintain more than twenty-six roads, or at least twenty-six main ones, thus they could be labeled A through Z. That's sound thinking to me, keeping the number of main roads to what's necessary. The short routes bear labels like "County Road BB" or even, for the most inconsequential lanes, "County Road BBB."

I've never stopped to go inside that Vikings/Packers borderline bar, which I passed some miles ago, but it's a kind of personal border for me. Minnesota, where I live now, means to me responsibilities and problems I can't do much about: Linda is angry at her younger son. Our house seems to attract more junk every year. The junk clutters not just our space but our lives. Our lives are busy with a lot of activities and concerns—like teenage sons who make us mad. It's a circle.

I'm a teacher who's just finished teaching for the year, and today, after I turn in my grades and pack the car, I'm off for a ramble by myself through Wisconsin, the place where I was born and raised and the landscape that is home. I feel first a depression that comes from shedding my nine-month life, one which I associate with Minnesota, however unfairly. It's the place I live now, the place that suggests to me what I've had to settle for. In my head many times I've written the essay: "Wisconsin and Minnesota, The Differences," and though they'd be subtle to a New Yorker, for us they're important as earth. That bar, for instance, with the line drawn down the middle: it wouldn't exist in Minnesota. Not because there are no Packer fans there, but because most people wouldn't take so seriously something which is so purely foolish.

The difference between Minnesota and Wisconsin is the difference between soybean fields and dairy farms. The former run flat and long, and the heat rises from them even in June, and the cicadas whir and the sun hangs in a blanched sky and the horizon goes on forever. Towns are islands, with more churches than bars (in the smallest towns maybe two churches— both Lutheran!—and no bars at all). People in auditoriums will think about it before they laugh too hard.

In Wisconsin, by contrast, dairy farms roll and rise. The essence of grass rises and mixes with sky, even in late summer. The smell of cow shit gets a joke out of the city people in their passing cars. People in bars, which out-number churches ten to one, will speak their minds, even if there's not much on their minds. The Lutherans don't seem as threatening in Wisconsin, since it's the damn Catholics you have to watch out for, our grandparents told us. We have a narrow sense of *we* that nevertheless on the best of days seems to include just about everybody.

Wisconsin to me now is the place I play in and the responsibilities are those I choose: what kind of six-pack to get for camping, do I need new line on my fishing reel, can I get there before the crowds set in, before Saturday, before July, or whenever? It's also the place of my past, the place I don't want to think about being not as good as it used to be. Nothing is as good as it used to be, except that it's better for whole groups of people who got screwed for hundreds of years, which is a good thing to have stopped. It's just too bad that as we finally realize everyone should have an equal shot at things, those things can't be as good for them as they used to be for a few people when things were bad for the rest. It's too bad the land can't live through what's happening to it, since everyone deserves a right to live closer to the land. That's not privilege, it's human sanity. It's also survival.

Evening: The moon is up. It's nearly a full moon, and it lights the open field as if in a science fiction story. The moon is white silver, and the evening dew simmers on the grass lying flat like long hair. Cold rises from the earth. It's a good feeling, because the cold helps me tell the difference between the body and what's outside of the body—like when you can see your breath. It's proof I exist and also that there is a real world outside of me.

Soon I must build myself a fire, something I've enjoyed since boyhood. I tear the label from a can of chili, taking the classified section from this morning's newspaper. I can find a few twigs that aren't wet with dew and I arrange them over the crumpled paper and light a match.

The small flames climb and gradually I place bigger and damper pieces of wood over the smoking fire. The moon rises now above the tallest tree on the edge of the field so that the light is a solid field over the field, unbroken now by the jigsaw shadows of branches. The water in the stream pours over rocks and down its course, making a sound that is not at all musical as the cliche would have it. The sound is formless, random, and inevitable. Music, in contrast, has form, the product of human agency. The sound of the stream is beyond human control. Thus it is superior to music, and since music is the greatest sound human beings can codify, there can be no name for this water sound in mere human terms.

Trout fishing is best carried out alone, so if you are your own worst enemy, as my mother always told me I was, you will need to sign an armistice, or negotiate a cease fire. The land is most itself when no one is present to take it in. With even one person there, it is violated, but that paradigm— one fisher, or one hiker, alone—is the closest the human animal can know to real solitude, of not existing except as part of the land. Perhaps if you're lucky you'll know that after death.

Getting There

My car climbs a hill through a rock cut, and down the other side lies the village of Colfax, with its white watertower like a golf ball on a tee at that country club a few miles back. It appears against a green hilly background. Across the way a herd of dairy cattle takes its time to be itself. In Colfax you can find "Karaoke with Dave: 5 p.m." at the Viking Bowl. You can find at least seven churches, the names of which are listed on the sign at the edge of town: United Methodist, First Lutheran, Church of Christ, and four more names I would have to stop moving to read. The Outhouse Bar lies a half a block from Railroad Street. "Colfax: Half Way Between the

Equator and the North Pole. 3186 Miles." It's one of many towns to boast of this. I wonder, if they had to leave, which way the residents would go, pole or equator? I like to think they'd go north. Just as Minnesota and Wisconsin carry meaning in my personal mythology, so do the concepts of north and south. North is fewer people, in more space, and weather designed to keep them out. North is a short growing season so that you can better appreciate every day of it. We shouldn't be able to control the weather. The weather is not supposed to be nice most of the time. Do I sound WASPy in this? Do I care? This is what North means, and thus exactly what South means is not very important because it can't mean this. Perhaps in Argentina, South means this. But Buenos Aires is a long way from the Halfway Bar and Karaoke with Dave.

Something about turning off a road onto a smaller road opens up possibilities, or gives the illusion of doing so. As I head towards the Singing Hills, the trees seem lighter in color, the season a bit behind up here, this little further north. It's like going back in time to earlier in the season, like being able to live a piece of life over again.

The Singing Hills don't sing to me, and in fact these hills are not really called the Singing Hills. I've seen a sign for a place in Southern Minnesota ("south" "Minnesota") called the Singing Hills, and although I like the name, I've never been there. It's probably flat and redolent of soybeans. This place in Wisconsin is called something else, but I'm not going to tell you what it is, because this is the place I turn off the road onto a smaller road. I don't want you around.

Most people do want you around, so stay with them. I want to keep my own company for these two days. The reason people are afraid of their own company is not loneliness, but that they're afraid of what they'll find. Having no companion to accommodate or annoy, they'll have to consider, just for a day or two, the person they've become. There will be no note to play off a lower note. I have a lot of sympathy for this brand of terror. The Singing Hills are a mirror in which you may not wish to see yourself.

✳

The Natural Superiority of Trout Fishing

Less Water. It stands to reason that it will be easier to find fish in a trout stream six feet wide than in a lake two miles long. In a small trout stream you can see or at least guess the architecture of the water: that stump, those rocks, the sun hitting it from such and such angle, evening growing over it from all sides like darkness must. You don't need fish locators, contour maps, or underwater cameras. You're not a submarine captain or a reconnaissance pilot; you're a trout fisherman.

Too much gear and too many gizmos is a bad thing in general. With any hobby it can be fun to collect its paraphernalia. But beware the accumulation of goods, which can clog the arteries of enjoyment, block the flow of the story like an accretion of detail. I prefer an ultralight rod and reel over a fly rod. I use small, horseshoe-shaped spoon called a Super Duper—a very old brand of lure and the one Tony Randall used in *Will Success Spoil Rock Hunter?*, though that in itself is no recommendation. If you're truly fishing in less water, and that water is surrounded by dense brush, which keeps other fishermen away, then you will not be able to use a fly rod anyway.

In general, old men with fly rods are probably OK. Young men with fly rods may be concerned with looking good as they use fly rods, concerned with catching the most fish they can because that's quality time so go for it. They may practice catch and release the way some people practice serial polygamy. They drive nice cars and fish once a year, usually on opening day. The rest of the time they golf. Good form.

When I am old, I shall wear waders. I shall use a fly rod.

Remember, you're your own worst enemy.

Now I can feel my mind starting to work for myself again after a long time of working for other people. I am tired of the world away from the trout steam, and so I try to choke off thoughts of that world now. There will be plenty of time to worry about home when I am back home. And there will be time tomorrow to go back and fish by morning the holes I fished late afternoon and evening today.

*

The ancient Greeks believed if you had jaundiced vision, seeing an oriole could restore you, even though your sighting would kill the bird. I heard that on AM radio on my drive to the trout stream yesterday.

This morning I saw two orioles in camp.

And last night for the first time in my life, I heard two whippoorwills calling at the same time. One was nearby, the other checking in from across the lake. There were clear skies and so it was a long dusk. The birds started their cry as soon as the sun went down, and because of the nearly full moon (full in two nights, my pocket calendar tells me), they went on through at least half the night. The moon was that bright, bright enough for me to read the smaller headlines on yesterday's paper before I crumpled it for the bed of my campfire. I know the whippoorwills cried at least half the night because at three, I heard the call again, this time right over my tent, so loud it woke me up. The bird called its own name, seemingly without pause, and not being able to get back to sleep, I rustled purposely, to scare that bird that before this night I had treasured hearing and had so rarely heard. I slid myself half out of the tent, and for the first time ever actually *saw* one of those reclusive birds—a dark, robin-sized clump settled against the branch of a birch tree on the peninsula where I was camped. But for three in the morning, this lovely bird was too close and loud. I knew that he could stand in one place and cry for twenty minutes, or even an hour. I shone my flashlight on his tree and made a small grunt. The bird flew away and I slid back into the tent for my moonless, silent sleep.

Loons, geese, barred owls (*"who cooks for you? who cooks for you all"*?) warblers, ducks. And in the middle of the road the next day, a bird with the breast of a robin, a long beak, and a mottled brown back. Round body like a softball, moving up and down steadily as in a dance to curse a sleeping child. Then it ran off into the brush on its long spindly legs. A male, judging by the color, he didn't call his name and I didn't know how to make his acquaintance.

When there are fewer people around, when there is a lower level of habitation of human beings per square mile, then running into someone can actually be a pleasure, or at least a benign experience: One finger off the steering wheel to wave through the window. You heading back to the car after an afternoon of fishing while the other party heads up stream the way you just came. "Get any?" "Just got a nice one about ten minutes ago." "Good luck."

But when there are too many of us, it's a constant game of hide and hope no one seeks. We can only live the inner life, which is based on the necessary fiction that we exist in a place by ourselves that is peaceful and sound. That's what humans who know enough to want it, want. We want to live in whatever degree of isolation is necessary for us to *choose* company—the when and the who and the where of it.

> "I confess to you that none of these three trout had to be beheaded, or folded double, to fit their casket. What was big was not the trout, but the chance. What was full was not my creel, but my memory."
> —ALDO LEOPOLD,
> *A Sand County Almanac*

*

Another Inconvenient Truth

In about 2050 the population of the US is projected to be as much as 500 million. That means for every two people you see now, there will be three people then. The kind of experience I'm having today will have become nearly impossible. Few who are living now take note of that fact. Most wouldn't even believe it's true. A few people—like some politicians, or those who can benefit from having a lot of other people around to work for low wages—will even get mad if they're reminded about this truth. It's OK to talk about climate change, but what is driving the change if not at base a population the earth was simply not meant to support?

So throughout the world, in addition to mass famine, wars over dwindling resources, a growing gap between rich and poor, there will be, once the crowd is here, nothing more that we now know as trout fishing. That's too bad. I also suspect that once we get to the point in time of all those people existing, breathing, fornicating, defecating, it will be the end of America. The country may still exist on a map (and we probably will have annexed Canada by then so we still have something left to pave over—manifest larceny), but I think the country as an idea will have ended by then. People are okay some of the time, even Americans, but it's hard to serve a meal of democracy, free speech, free enterprise, and the like, at a table with so many chairs. It's easier to eat on the run, and so we will.

Even now, most of the world with no people in it—call it wilderness, the frontier, open space, the countryside, whatever—is gone. We will be the last generation to have the outdoors at hand, relatively speaking, yet still unspoiled, relatively speaking. And even though we know only the remnants of the wilderness that we call the outdoors, like scraps of cloth cut from a larger national, natural flag, we're still lucky that we can get to some of these places with ease—a smaller road off a larger road. Because we are the last generation to have this gift, it is our responsibility to fight against its passing, and then bear witness to its passing so that people in the future will have some idea about what they have been cheated out of, nothing less than what life was supposed to be.

There is a time to clean out your senses, to see and hear closely enough, up to the capacity that a human being has. There is so much distraction. It's good fortune to be a teacher and have time in May to get away when no one else can. It's best to work Saturday and Sunday, and make Monday through Friday the Lord's days and head out to the woods then, out to the Lord's temple, when you're much less likely to see anyone there—not even the Lord.

*

The Natural Superiority of Trout Fishing

Trouble you avoid by not lake fishing. Fishing from shore there's always a chance some asshole is going to pull up a lawn chair right next to your stump, or crowd on to the pier or dock with you. Is there any question that the worst kind of fishing is being lined up along some small-town public access with every know-it-all in the county, and you're the only one who doesn't chew, or who didn't bring the kids, or who can properly conjugate a verb?

Maybe you aren't your own worst enemy after all.

In a boat, as the hours pass, you have to deal with your back getting tired and doing its best to replicate a piece of cooked lasagna. You have to deal with idiots in powerboats and on water skis who think of small fishing boats the way test drivers think of those orange cylindrical cones they're supposed to avoid knocking over. And worse yet you have to deal with people on "personal watercraft." Is there any question in the mind of a reasonable fisherman that these floating chainsaws, these radiation-enhanced mosquitoes, should be made illegal? Or perhaps we could choose one state—say, Kansas—flood it, and just *give* it to these people who want to zoop around in and make a lot of racket on otherwise nice days. Personal watercraft are not personal, which is why they're offensive. They are to lakes what botulism is to canned soup.

Fishing in a boat, you have to endure the guys who pass you in their fishing boat and ask, "Catch anything?" and then you have to lie. Either that or make up some folksy sounding, self-effacing reply that reveals essentially nothing like, "Not in this weather, hey" or "A few small ones, but nothing to brag about"—this on days everyone in your party had been knocking them dead.

> "All fishermen are liars, except you and me, but
> sometimes, I'm not so sure about you."
>
> —ANONYMOUS

✳

It was the kind of day on the stream when all the fish seemed to be in moving water, or if in still water, then at the edge of the rapids. I was getting action on almost every cast on which I was able to drop my Super Duper into a logical spot. One fish, the first, was nine inches long (they're all brook trout here), which is one inch more than the legal minimum here, and the smallest I will keep. I'd had the drag on my little spinning reel set too light, since I'd put on new line the night before and goofed up the setting. I was reeling the fish back through the rapids, not making any progress, so I had to haul him in by moving the pole up and to the side, then grabbing the end of the line, and repeating the motion till the brookie was on the bank. Glad there was no one here to see that.

Nine inches doesn't sound like a big trout, but consider that this stream is about eight feet wide, and only two or three feet deep in most places, and even in spring the deepest holes don't run five feet. While I'm alive, I'm happy to live according to this scale. Bringing in a ten- or twelve-inch trout with ultra-light gear in a stream this small is good kicks.

The second brookie was one of those fin stretchers: Eight and three quarters, eight and seven eighths. I put him on the rack and made him nine since he was hooked deeply and probably would have died anyway, and I was anxious to get the limit of three trout allowed me. It wasn't out of some fisherman's pride that I wanted three trout; it's because three trout would be enough for my supper back at camp.

The next fish was the often-chronicled one who got away. I wasn't even sure I had a fish on the line at first. It felt like a snag—a dull tug on the line instead of the usual grab and run, when you can actually feel the muscle of the fish on your line. This one must have just taken a look at my Duper, and it hooked him loosely through the lip. But then as soon as he was hooked, my drag was whining, straining against the power of the fish, even set tight now. I got a look only at the side of the fish as it surfaced for a second. It looked the size of a nice bass. And as soon as that he was gone. Later, I was resigned to the idea that the two smaller fish and a piece of sausage I'd brought from home would be supper. I'd already turned back to the car when I decided to take a couple shots at a hole in which I'd had some action on the way in.

Bang—first cast, a big one putting up a fight. I reeled him in quickly—eleven and a half inches, a nice trout in this little stream.

That night, the fish tasted good. I cooked and ate the two smaller ones first, left the third one on to cook longer. I can almost always catch fish on this stretch of stream I'm not telling you the name of.

I wasn't embarrassed giving a silent thanks for my meal and the day. I would not be back until fall.

In graduate school I had a professor who had us read the *Collected Stories of Ernest Hemingway*, and the book to me, with its clarity of purpose and economy of means, seemed better than the Hemingway novels I'd read earlier. I don't know how I'd react to Papa's writing now—with its masculine excesses, its style so given to parody. I haven't gone back there either.

The professor was a man only a bit older than I am now who seemed very old to me at the time. He was short and round, flowing hair gray at the temples. He smoked a curved pipe, wore dark-rimmed glasses and pastel sweater vests, and his hobby was making furniture, I was told. I was in school in Arizona, and though there were likely trout streams up in the mountains, I was not in a fishing period of my life, and was too taken up by the desert and my studies to investigate.

Most of us had already read "The Big Two-Hearted River" as younger students, and now the professor, who was a pretty good teacher my friends and I thought, was recounting the story. Nick Adams leaps out of the baggage car at the site of an Upper Michigan town consumed by fire. He studies the river below a railroad bridge, hikes into the hills, and is hyper-aware of his surroundings: charred stumps, summer heat over a pine plain, and especially a gaggle of grasshoppers, all sooty black.

Hemingway reports the spare details of Nick's observations, and insists repeatedly that the young man is happy. Nick sets up camp, eats onion sandwiches, sleeps. The next day he fishes for trout. There is almost no mention of the world away from the river.

"It's apparent to me," my professor concludes, "that Nick Adams, this veteran of the Great War, is a young man on the verge of a nervous breakdown." The professor gestured aptly with the curved pipe, then sat back into his chair at the seminar table.

"Nervous breakdown." It was a phrase that even then was passing into disuse, and I remember being surprised at the drama of the teacher's conclusion about so understated a story—so surprised that I didn't know if I agreed with him or not. He'd no doubt used the line before in other classes. He was nearing retirement, and would spend those years making rockers and end tables, not hopping freights and camping near burned away towns.

Years beyond the teacher with the pipe, I was reading a book by the Dalai Lama in which he wrote of the need for family planning even though "some of the latest studies suggest a population implosion a century from now." I wondered what his sources were, but there were no notes to the book. Would the implosion occur before the opening day of fishing season? Or would the blessed break come only in time to improve things from unlivable to just awful?

"As a monk," His Holiness adds in the book, "it's perhaps inappropriate for me to comment on these matters." I guessed that, like Hemingway, this was more understatement open to interpretation.

Once a friend of mine went up to Michigan to fish Hemingway's Big Two-Hearted River, and to write a piece about it for an outdoor magazine. My friend discovered that the real Big Two-Hearted runs nowhere near the burned town outside of which Hemingway placed Nick's camping spot. As a young man, after the war, Hemingway had fished another river up in Michigan. He apparently liked the Big Two-Hearted name so borrowed it. His description of the river was uncannily accurate, my friend reported. But as far as anyone knows, Hemingway never laid eyes on the real Two-Heart. When he wrote the story, he was living in Paris.

✳

A List of Common Streamside Wildflowers

> "As we return to a happier equilibrium (between industrialism and a rural-agrarian way of life) we will of course also encourage a gradual reduction of the human population of these states to something closer to the optimum: perhaps half the present number."
> —EDWARD ABBEY,
> *Freedom and Wilderness,*
> *Wilderness and Freedom,* 1977

Morning. I got out of the tent and was still rubbing the last night's campfire smoke out of my eyes. It was late; I'd slept long, still tired from the drag of the Minnesota world. A white-tailed deer had come up the road to the tip of this peninsula on which I'd camped. He saw me, turned tail and ran. It was a nice way to start the day, just as the big fish had been a nice way to end the previous day. I couldn't believe my luck in seeing so much wildlife in so short a time away from people, that other species.

Last night: the moon rising, the sun setting—I knew it would probably be the last time I'd see a clear sky on this trip. The yellow light from the long sun shone across the bay on the birch, aspen, and maple trees on that shore. And above the shoreline a few degrees the nearly full moon rising.

This day, trout fishing, I bring my wildflower guidebook in a fanny pack: Marsh marigold (leaves large as salad leaves, six-fingered yellow hand), bunchberry, large-flowered trillium ("trillions," we misheard the prolific name as kids), painted trillium, common strawberry, starflower, phlox, Jack-in-the-pulpit (note the drops of dew or rain around the sermon), common blue violet, true forget-me-not, dwarf ginseng, swamp buttercup, showy lady's slipper, spring beauty.

And the trout lily: "This is one of our most common spring wildflow-ers....the name refers to the similarity between the leaf markings and those of the brown or brook trout."

If we value what is scarce, and human life is truly sacred, should we not then make less of it? And yet in this placement of these streamside wildflow-ers, random yet with a reason and purpose, it's the abundance that inspires in the observer that very human desire to make a list. It's a way to appreciate and lend order, still respectful of the distance between that which is of us and that which is around us.

II

The Baker Boys: A Fable ===

I FOUND MY COPY OF *THE FABULOUS BAKER BOYS* IN MY BOX OF OLD DVDs in the basement. We're at home mid-pandemic, and Linda and I are looking for a comedy to watch tonight, but something with a bite and with some subtext.

We know this movie will fill the bill, at least if our memory—OK, my memory—hasn't fooled us again. Yes, the cover copy on the case reminds me, the film was made more than thirty years ago, so it's been a while. A lot of things that seem to me like they just recently happened, didn't. The passing of the years means that most people now haven't seen the film, but then, not many people saw it in 1989, either.

I'll fill you in on the important stuff as I go...and some of the less important stuff as well. For example, that the film's most noted scene in its day was the one in which a young Michelle Pfeiffer, clad in a slinky cocktail dress, sings "Makin' Whoopee" while sprawling and crawling all over Jeff Bridges' grand piano. Today we'd call the scene "hot," even though that term didn't exist at that time of production. The scene is sexy, even witty (someone should write about the intersection of those two descriptors.) It was actually choreographed, the credits tell us. But despite the raves of critics and viewers of that day, the scene is not what's proven important about the film.

What *is* important: it's the best film Hollywood ever made about working musicians. I say "important," but maybe no one else cares. If no one does, don't tell me, since I've occasionally been a working musician and more often wanted to think of myself as one. It's also true that that lack of caring is what the film is about.

I grant you that the milieu of the film is dated: two lounge lizard pianists, approaching middle age, stuff themselves into tuxes to play hokey music in hotel bars, at weddings, on telethons—essentially any place that will pay them, barely adequately, at the end of the night. That part of the music scene has mostly disappeared. A plot summary would tell you that these two pianists, who happen to be brothers, have been playing together for thirty-one years. That Frank (played by Beau Bridges, Jeff's brother) handles the business side of the act—practical, a husband and father, a guy with a mortgage—while Jack is the artist-who-never-was, the guy who could never make the leap to set out in the uncertain world. He lives in a seedy apartment, womanizing, drowning his disappointments.

At the start of the story, even the practical brother can see that the world is changing around their act. "Two pianos isn't enough anymore," says Frank. "It never was," Jack adds.

So Frank decides to add a singer to the act, and the Michelle Pfeiffer character Susie is as appealing as she is unpolished. But the duo cum trio takes off and starts to pack every lounge they play. Of course Jack and Susie are attracted to each other and if you've been to the movies at all, you know the rest.

The film is what Graham Greene might have called "an entertainment," and its charm exists at the intersection of several genres and conventions. Which is to say it deals in cliches and types, as Hollywood can do so well. It's *Künstler* cinema: from the German for the story of the long-suffering artist lost in a commercial culture that ignores his talent. Tightlipped, disillusioned Jack is redeemed by the prostitute with the heart of gold, another venerable trope. When asked at audition, Susie says her only previous entertainment experience is having been on call for the AAA Escort Service.

The two brothers are two halves of the perfect whole—one responsible, one creative. One practical and uncomplicated, one moody and indecipherable. And *voila*, instant conflict. The rising action culminates in the second plot point, right where Hollywood says it should be, about 90 minutes into a two-hour feature, when the brothers have a physical scrap in an alley. They fight like brothers, so it's mostly pushing and shoving. You knew that was coming, too, but you didn't mind when it arrived. You could almost have written it yourself.

So... gritty and realistic? *Verité*? It occurs to me instead that the Latin root of the "Fabulous" of the title—*fabula*—is the same as that of "fable." A short tale that conveys a moral. A myth. As the name of the brothers' act, "fabulous" denotes the commercial oversell, the hype. "Branding" we would call it these thirty years later, when artists are required to *be* Frank, always selling themselves along with their work. If Jack the artist can survive the puffery, the expanding of the brand, so much the better. But that's not guaranteed, nor is it necessary.

Whatever the current word for this promotion, we've known the concept for an eternity as "bullshit."

The appeal of the film is that the fable in the other sense of the word, the myth of the misunderstood artist, holds so much truth. The bored, talented Jeff Bridges at the keyboard could be Kafka, Emily Dickinson, Van Gogh and the early impressionists, or just about any jazz musician ever. We see the brothers play terrible gigs and cringe for both of them. The blender behind the bar during a tender ballad. The laughing-too-loud drunk in an empty room near the close of the last set. The telethon on channel 71 at 3 a.m., raising money for a high school gymnasium. No one is watching. And no one need listen. Jack says near the movie's climax that for thirty-one years, from the moment he got on stage each night with Frank, he couldn't wait for the gig to end.

If the film had been made later, we might also see something of the path that led the talented singer Susie to her lot in life. The instructive story, even with the Hollywood unlikelihoods of the plot, will simply ring true.

The audience identifies with Jack, for in life as in art, the film suggests we all play these "bad gigs." We all face disappointment, misunderstanding, have had the crummy jobs. Reality unceasingly demands compromise, and how much to give? There's simply too much crossing and recrossing at the busy intersections of life, people walking all six ways at once without time to look back before the light changes. We all know the particulars, have lived them. The world that's preoccupied with its own survival has little time for one person's goals and desires, no matter how faithfully and sincerely pursued. Bogart says something like that at the end of *Casablanca*. He was talking about love, but most art is love. Isn't it?

Yet somehow, we soldier on, persevere. Why do we do that? More importantly, how do we do that? It's not easy, the film reminds us.

*

All jazz musicians love to tell their "worst gig ever" stories, which is perhaps why *The Fabulous Baker Boys* speaks so clearly to my tribe. My piano player Larry likes to recount his time as a sideman for an Elvis impersonator, which put him through college. The pay was steady, but the beige polyester jump suits got a bit close on stage. My own worst gig might have been getting booked, one assumes by mistake, with an R&B band into a small-town country music bar. The proprietor agreed to pay most of what he owed us if we would just agree to leave. Also a time early on when a drunken dancer crashed into my music stand mid-set, almost wiping out the new saxophone my parents had just paid for.

My college jazz band director may have had the best of these tales ever. He was in a stage band and one of the acts featured a guy with two trained donkeys. It was probably a county fair. The band would play those familiar opening strains of Strauss's "Blue Danube" waltz, the most famous of Viennese melodies, later borrowed in that scene with the orbiting spacecraft in *2001: A Space Odyssey. du DU da da DAH,* the band played… and then the animal trainer, standing behind the donkeys and smiling, would squeeze, in time, the donkeys' testicles, and each would oblige with the next two notes on cue, one higher pitched, the next lower: HEE HEE. HAW HAW.

du DU da da DAH…. HEE HEE. HAW HAW.

Is this a true story? *Could* it be? Not sure that truth is the point of the telling. What I want to tell you about those "worst gig ever" stories instead is this: I very much regret that I didn't collect more of my own. Maybe it's just for the sake of having the stories to tell. Call it another myth if you will. The romance of being able to make a buck playing music, no matter how unde-sirable the venue. It's the joy of being able to say, "This is how I started," and here I am now.

For now I'm at an age at which a person becomes more aware of time left than of time already lived. I regret that I didn't keep up my piano lessons, that I never mastered a foreign language, that I didn't attend a top ranked college. And if I had only learned bass guitar, I could have gigged much much more on weekends over the years.

But I also regret not playing in that stage band with my teacher, or in that empty tiki lounge playing "Girl From Ipanema" for the hundredth time with Frank and Jack.

✳

I'm writing from the midst of the pandemic, winter '20/'21. Eleven months into the long slog, with no sure end in sight. We are all in crisis mode again, in isolation that has brought, along with many other more important things, a drastic reduction of work for musicians. Because everyone in my jazz quartet is COVID-responsible, and we're at an age where we can't afford to risk getting the virus, our last gig came almost two months ago. It came about because we were blessed with a mild and long autumn this year in Minnesota. Three days before Christmas, with the temperature still hover-ing close to 40 degrees (!) and no snow yet on the ground, the four of us donned our gay apparel—fleeces and vests, boots and stocking caps—and set up in Larry-the-piano-player's back yard to videorecord a concert. I brought a couple handwarmers to keep in my pockets, the kind people use for deer hunting.

Larry invited the neighbors, set up a couple good mics, a pocket cam-era and his cell phone to capture the event, to release on YouTube a couple nights later. We knew from having played this "room" earlier in the pan-demic that the arrangement of houses and garages on the alley was such that the acoustics would be surprisingly good.

It had been three months since the four of us last played together. We gathered in the backyard mid-afternoon, when the drummer's day job schedule allowed him to get away. With the end of the short winter day before us and temperatures falling, we didn't have time to rehearse. Just set up, tune up, and, *bang,* start to play. Folks strolled up the alley and gathered on lawn chairs and even sat on what this late in the year in St. Paul could barely be described as lawn. Larry's wife started a campfire.

The recording tells the true story: we played beautifully, aided as we were by an occasional barking neighbor dog, or chirping chickadee, or far-off siren. At one point Linda was passing to her seat and didn't duck low enough under the eye of the camera, and her back shows up in the frame. At another point between tunes, I sighed and said, "Gee, I didn't realize how much I *missed* all this, missed playing I mean."

"Richard," one of the guys replied, "you *are* playing. Right now."

More truth.

The next day a heavy snow arrived and winter in Minnesota set in. We collected a few bucks from the YouTube concert and donated it to the local homeless shelter.

I knew there would be no work now, with winter here. I faced the prospect of practicing intermittently and hearing my facility on the saxophone inevitably decline with each passing week. It was a depressing notion, in an already down time, and I wanted to spare myself the loneliness of playing less well each time I took out the horn. For me, practicing is no substitute for rehearsal, and rehearsal is no substitute for performance, not in an improvised art. From the time forward when I learned not to be nervous on stage, I've always thrived on that connection with listeners. Since it's jazz, just a few people will suffice and they don't have to be listening all that closely. Just be in the moment with us. And OK, I admit I don't enjoy practicing that much.

The Fabulous Baker Boys ends with Frank and Jack breaking up after the thirty-one years. And admit it, you knew that was going to happen, too. Frank will make just as much money teaching lessons to neighborhood kids in his suburb. As for Jack, earlier in the story we saw him sit in at the local dark and smoky jazz club, playing a tune of his own composition. Since this is Hollywood, the tune doubles as the soundtrack for the unfolding story. It's a gorgeous piece—dark, evocative. Jack's pain is in the lines of melody, and in the color of the muted trumpet and tenor sax that play the theme in the score. As I watch the film, I can't forget that Larry and I performed "Jack's Theme" many times as a jazz duo, even recorded it on a CD.

Hearing it again in its original context makes rise in me the kinds of feelings that only music can engender—that beauty in the face of diminished hope, that thing that's in us and has to come out. It's like not needing to cry. It's a sigh. Quiet joy reveling in our own impossibilities.

At the very end of *The Fabulous Baker Boys*, Jack and Susie decide that yes, they'll see each other again. And more importantly, the owner of the local jazz club tells Jack simply, "I have Tuesdays and Thursdays open."

That's the moral of the story, the artist wanting the night to never, ever end.

I haven't touched my horn now for forty-one days. It's already mid-February. But if I start practicing tomorrow, by the time the temperature hits forty degrees again, and the March slush is flowing down gutters to storm sewers and raising the Mississippi River to the crest of its banks. By the time the sun is higher and, some afternoons at least, brighter in the sky. By that time, we can set up again on Larry's driveway. We'll wear layers. We'll think about clubs and bars reopening. How anxious, how crazy people will be to get out. Each listener will be in the midst of his or her own personal first day of spring.

If I start playing now, I can be ready. They'll want to hear everything.

Making New from Old ===

THE GREAT JAZZ TRUMPETER MILES DAVIS CLAIMED HE NEVER LIS-
tened to his own old recordings. That's why his CD with Quincy
Jones, *Miles and Quincy Live at Montreux* in 1991 was hailed as such
an exceptional occasion. The liner notes talk of Miles' "stubborn refusal to
relive his early years." "Miles was always looking ahead," his fellow players
testified.

As much as anyone, I enjoy the nostalgia captured on that live Montreux
concert disc, when Miles returns to his material of as much as forty years
before: *Boplicity, Porgy and Bess, Miles Ahead.* The nostalgia is deepened
when one knows that only four weeks later, Miles would be admitted to the
hospital for pneumonia, and perhaps for exhaustion at sixty-five years of life
as Miles Davis. He was never discharged.

But I disagree with most of the critical appraisals of the CD: I don't think
Miles sounds all that good on the new recording. He was sick and weak, but
I doubt that's the reason. I wonder if maybe Miles was right all along *not*
to revisit ground he had already covered—in some cases years before anyone else had ever thought of going there. Miles' recording of "Boplicity" in
about 1957 sounds *newer* to me than his recording of the same arrangement in 1991. Maybe one of the greatest artists of the century was essentially
right: sure, you *could* go home again, but why bother? Especially if the whole
musical world, the world of the *new* could be your residence.

Miles never listened to any of his own old recordings. A week or so ago
the radical nature of that statement occurred to me: Miles *never* listened to
any of his own old recordings. He never heard some of the great American

music of the last century, just because he had recorded it. It reminds me of the late Beethoven who could hear his ninth symphony only in his head, and on occasions at the end of his career would go on conducting his music with his eyes closed unaware that the orchestra had stopped playing. All of Vienna laughed.

Or perhaps Dick Cavett's appraisal of Groucho Marx, that Groucho was often depressed simply because he was the only one in the world who didn't have a Groucho Marx to cheer him up. He couldn't listen to himself since it just wouldn't sound the same as it did to everyone else.

I've listened to Miles' *Kind of Blue* album hundreds of times. If what they say is true, after about 1960, Miles never listened to it at all.

We can learn a lot from listening to ourselves, musically or in life, but we can also take a lesson from the masters, and just keep going. We make new from old, which is to say from experience. If you think of it, what choice do we have? Young people may try to make new from new; for most of those not young, that won't resonate, due to the truth that experience teaches, that there is very little new under the sun.

It's just as true that, as Nick Carraway told Gatsby, "You can't repeat the past." Think of that Jorge Borges story in which a writer rewrites *Don Quixote* word for word and insists that because he's writing it at a different time and place, he's made something new and something that is *his* art, not Cervantes'. The story is like a joke that's funny because of how really smart it is.

Miles Davis was famous for not giving his musicians much advance notice of what tunes were going to be played on a gig, or even on a recording session. On one studio date you can hear Miles' gravelly voice instructing before one tune, "I'll play it, and tell you what it is later." For the session for *Kind of Blue*, considered by many to be the most important jazz album ever made, Miles didn't even write out the music, but merely brought in sketches for what everybody was supposed to play "because I wanted a lot of spontaneity." One of the other musicians on the date recalls that Miles was still giving instructions when the tape had already begun to roll.

How different this is from the practice of those old pop and rock groups that tour into old age and beyond, playing at the local casino or even the country fair, the band made up of maybe one or two, or maybe none of the original members. The music is music in name only, its marketing become the real performance.

For the rest of us the tape is still rolling. The page or canvas is blank, the air silent with possibilities.

WHO WAS BILL EVANS? ══════

START Here

1. his music, like his personality, had a questioning quality

2. he wasn't a narcissist, apparently

3. he sought the essence of the material in its harmonic implications

4. Miles Davis said, "It's a drag he's dead. Now I'll never get to hear him play 'Alfie' again"

5. he started as a flute player

6. he didn't live as long as he might have otherwise; he didn't live to be old

7. whereas many people don't eat properly when they're kids, he didn't eat properly at the end of his life. Malnutrition was listed as a contributing cause of death. Coffee. Also cocaine

8. he loved to golf, bowl

9. his long-time girlfriend Ellaine threw herself in front of a subway train in 1970

10. he had lifelong feelings of inadequacy

11. he played early on with saxist Herbie Fields, whose career ended tragically in suicide

12. he was left-handed, which may account in part for his chordal proficiency

13. he wasn't African American, and he never resided permanently in a foreign country to escape racial prejudice at home

14. at his death, Oscar Peterson said, "Maybe he found what he was looking for"

15. he knew a great deal about the novels of Thomas Hardy and the poetry of William Blake

16. loan sharks threatened to break his hands

17. he said, "I had to work harder at music than most cats because, you see, man, I don't have very much talent."

✳

Thesis

Why would one of the great artists of his day be so self-destructive as to kick a heroin habit only to start a cocaine habit? "When I get into something, I really get into it," he is known to have said. Does that explain?

Shortly before his death he told his young bass player how amazed he was at the insidiousness of his new drug.

We can read that his life was a fifty-year-long suicide. We can read that he was a nice man, had a sense of humor better than your grandfather's, wanted a child and when he had one thought his life was complete, then moved out from his family. Dying of cocaine, he thought he was happy.

Some jazz musician junkies played the music only to get money to score. Chet Baker would forget his trumpet on a bandstand in his haste to shoot up. Charlie Parker had to borrow money for cab fare. But Bill Evans practiced constantly. "I heard him practice Ravel, Debussy," his wife Nenette said after his death, "but I never heard him practice jazz."

He said, "You don't understand. It's like death and transfiguration. Every day you wake in pain like death and then you go out and score, and that is transfiguration. Each day becomes all of life in microcosm."

❋

Leaving my footprints
    nowhere
        south or north
I go into hiding
here by the bay full of moonlight...

Muso Seki (W. S. Merwin, translator)

❋

Bill Evans is given credit for inventing the jazz piano trio. Think about it: no blaring horns, no chick singer, nothing to dance to. A piano is an instrument that can't color or bend tones. What it is, it is. It's so common as to be in every parlor or basement, so playing it is like making poetry from the words printed on a menu or a cereal box.

In the years between Sinatra and the Beatles, Bill Evans formulated a new jazz instrument consisting of three people joined at the beat—piano, bass, and drums. This rough beast was amorphous, something to be agreed on, not timed.

And of the three players, it was the bassist and the pianist who most played as if from the same body. It's not you play what I play, which would be an untrained listener's first assumption. It's you anticipate what I'm about to play based on what I'm playing right this second, what I've played since the tune has begun, what we've played in all the nights/years we've worked together, and on the basis of everyone who's ever played or recorded this tune.

And of the trios Bill Evans led, it was his first, with bassist Scott LaFaro, that was the most prescient, where the piano and bass first melded into this new animal. No one accompanied anyone else. Rather, partners.

Play something that you think will fit perfectly—not too obviously, not unsubtly—with what you think I'll play. Surprise me. But don't get in the way, don't piss me off.

The audience? Are there people sitting out there? OK, they're allowed to listen over our shoulders.

They don't understand.

Then LaFaro was killed in a car wreck, aged 25. Bill Evans was 31.

✳

His Reluctance

"The trouble with Bill—and, as much as anything, that was the cause for our deciding to record him live—was always persuading Bill to play at all."

—ORIN KEEPNEWS

"Of course, Bill would never have let any work out at all if he wasn't compelled to support a career."

—NENETTE EVANS

"It is a peculiarity of mine that despite the fact that I am a professional performer … I have always preferred playing without an audience."

—BILL EVANS

✳

You Don't Understand

Bopsters of the fifties often took up heroin because Charlie Parker used it (even though Bird said dope never made anyone play better). We listeners like to plug in the sociological explanation that the racism of the day drove these great but disrespected artists to despair.

Bill Evans was white. ("He was a punk," said Stanley Crouch, an African American critic, years after this death.) While he was often broke, he never lacked for work except when his habit got out of hand.

The pain is in the music. That much we can hear, especially in the ballads he was famous for. Why do we assume that the life of someone who was a great artist should be more easily explained than the mystery of our own experience? A fact is not sound. A collection of facts does not necessarily carry the logic of music, or even the music of logic.

Biography is tyranny.

*

The White Tuxedo

One story has it that near the end of his life, performing at the Village Vanguard, he showed up late for the gig, dressed in a white tuxedo and eating a chocolate popsicle. He was in a bad state, but played beautifully, all but unaware as the chocolate melted over the keyboard.

*

"The Perplexity of Never Knowing Things for Certain"

A typical audition with Bill Evans' trio would have the candidate come down to some place like the Village Vanguard and sit in for the entire night. At the end of the evening, the pianist would say nothing. Maybe a pleasantry, a nod of the head.

He rehearsed his trios only a handful of times in his twenty-one years leading them. It wasn't necessary for him to tell his bassist and drummer what tune they were about to play and in what key. He just started playing.

He also apparently never wrote a set list in advance of a performance. He did, however, once copy down on a bar napkin for a young pianist in the audience the chord changes for a new composition he had just performed in the previous set.

That's it. He'll call you.

I'm a jazz saxophonist. My drummer and I have a running joke. In days past, when either of us would sub on a gig with some bandleader we didn't know, especially older guys, "ear guys," who play everything without a page of music in front of them, the bandleader would call a tune by name, but not tell you anything about it. He never said, "When you get to the B section, the changes go up in fourths, and then there's a Latin thing happening..." Nothing like that. Instead the leader would simply say,

"Don't worry, you'll hear it."

And sometimes you would hear it. But there would be that moment of uncertainty when you didn't know if you would hear it, and what would you play then? That was the worry.

Perhaps that's where art resides, or maybe this moment merely marks the difference between professional and amateur.

But that's the punch line of our joke: you'll hear it. Someone in our band brings in a chart to rehearsal: "it's in 9/4 time, kind of a tango, I wrote it for the funeral of my aunt."

And the drummer and I say together, "Don't worry, you'll hear it."

⁕

Who Owns the Silence?

The central problem is that there's so little work for jazz musicians right now. It's the weak economy, everyone says, though they offer that as the rationale for anything: bad weather, impotence, a taste for chocolates.

That and the fact that jazz popularity (to the degree that jazz is ever popular) goes in cycles. Right now, we're at a low point in the cycle, when people who wouldn't be listening anyway don't particularly think it's cool to go to a club or bar where local jazz musicians play.

Or club owners think that their customers think this way. And so if you look at the calendar for one of the few jazz clubs in my city, you see R&B on a Tuesday, a Klezmer/rock fusion on Thursday, a few national acts blowing through town ("song writer Jimmy Webb," "The New Soul Review," Lucinda Williams), and the rest of the week chick singers singing what Sinatra stopped singing years before he died, in the last century. But at the best jazz club in my city, instrumental jazz is seldom on the schedule, and that performed by local players like me and my band mates, almost never.

I drive friends through town and point out the places I used to play (seventy-five, maybe a hundred bucks a guy, one free drink) which are now closed or have cut out music: 1. Rossi's—belly up. 2. The joint on Washington—it's now a tiki bar. 3. Café Luxx—there's still a graphic of two saxophones among the letters painted on the window outside the bar: *Café L-U- sax-sax.* But no live music inside.

I can even drive past a church we played that's now closed.

Jazz? "Don't worry you'll hear it." Or you used to.

✳ .

Telling the Difference

Of the four black men in the Miles Davis Quintet of 1959, John Coltrane is the one who most objected to having a white man at the piano. Bill Evans eventually left Miles partly because of the racial tensions among the band members, but went back for a studio session once when Miles asked him to come back. That session became *Kind of Blue*, generally held to be the greatest jazz album ever.

"We just really went in that day and did our thing," he said.

If you're white and leading a regular life in this century, it's hard to imagine what it must have been like to be a genius and black in 1959. Bill Evans had to imagine it then. Hair slicked back, dark-framed glasses, cardigan sweater buttoned up, puffy young face, quiet. He looked more like an accountant than a jazz musician. Everyone said that.

Upon joining the group, Evans was told by Miles that there was one small matter of initiation: "You have to fuck everybody in the band." Bill walked away and thought about it for fifteen minutes and returned. "I'm sorry, I don't think I could do that."

(He had a sense of humor better than your grandfather's.)

"My man," Miles laughed.

In 1992, before a rerelease of *Kind of Blue*, an astute engineer discovered that on the first three cuts of one day of recording, the tape had been running slow so that on every pressing of the album to that point, some of the music was about a quarter step sharp.

For over thirty years, no critic or player or listener had noticed the difference.

❉

On the Need for a Sound Business Plan

Larry, the piano player I work with, says that people opening a bar or restaurant should ask the musicians whether or not the business will fail. We can tell right off. One place, a wine bar and adjacent deli, offered to pay the musicians only in coupons for their own establishment: seventy-five dollars in credit, plus a free (nice) dinner and all you cared to drink. Fine, we did the gig.

But then the next time we played the place it was fifty bucks in coupons, and you could have a pizza or salad but not the main entry, one glass of wine. Well, OK....

The last time we played there it was fifty bucks in coupons, and go hungry and bring a flask. I used some of my credit from previous gigs at the deli and got home to find I'd bought moldy cheese and stale crackers. Some overpriced canned soup.

I was about to go to the place with Linda to use more of my stash of coupons. I checked the bar's web site only to read that the place was closing in a week. No surprise to the musicians. So I called Larry, who'd played there more than me. Larry ate dinner there every night for the following week, just to use up his credit with the joint before it folded. It was the principle of the thing. He brought his friends, maybe an ex-girlfriend. Maybe bought drinks for strangers.

❉

Scott LaFaro

"While we were listening to the tape, Bill was a wreck, and he kept saying something like 'Listen to Scott's bass, it's like an organ! It sounds so big, it's not real, it's like an organ, I'll never hear that again.'

"Bill continued to play 'I Loves You, Porgy' over and over again, almost obsessively—but almost always as a solo number.

"After LaFaro's death, Bill was like a man with a lost love, always looking to find its replacement."

—GENE LEES

＊

A Controversy

Ken Burns made a nineteen-hour series for public TV on the history of jazz. In the series, Burns spent two entire two-hour episodes on two-year periods in the 1930s, a decade in which jazz was at the height of its popularity, but perhaps a low point in innovation and complexity. To the last forty years of jazz in the twentieth century Burns devoted one episode only.

In the entire series, Bill Evans' music is discussed for ninety seconds. None of his music, other than from Miles' *Kind of Blue* is played.

＊

A True Story

The speaker, an African American poet, asks for a show of hands. How many of the fifty-odd college students attending this lecture on the intersection of music and writing know who Bill Evans was? No one raises a hand.

The poet reads a reminiscence about his father hearing Bill Evans play at a Black club on the South side of Chicago in the 1950s ("That white mutha-fucka can flat-out play.") Behind his words a pianist plays a skillful imitation of Bill Evans.

In her playing, I can hear the close, impressionistic voicings, as if Debussy had done drugs and lived, as if Satie had set newspaper advertise-ment copy to music just yesterday, and not a hundred years ago, as he did. I'm probably the only one in the audience who can hear this in her playing. The college students in the audience can't hear it.

I hear the woman's variations of touch on the keys, the implied rubato that nonetheless offers a pulse and a pace. Listening to her is like walking through a gallery at the Met and seeing a student with an easel set up before a Vermeer. The yellows and blues against a dark background. The poetry of composition—light rhyming with light. That not caring too much, done so carefully. We watch the student before the master and smile quietly, since this brings us a warm feeling about the continuities in art, and by extension in life, that what is great is rare and will always be. That great art, copied by one, is better than bad art embraced by all.

How to describe music, anyway?

As if Ravel had given in to his late desire to play jazz, which he loved....

Jazz bandleader Stan Kenton told a story about himself as a kid, trying to sneak into a Paris club to hear jazz. He was too young to drink, even in France. The concierge finally said, OK, just go sit in the corner with that old man. His name is Maury.

And it went like this for several evenings. Go sit in the corner with Maury, kid.

Years later, Kenton learned that the old man had been Maurice Ravel.

"The questions I might have asked...," Kenton mused.

After the poetry reading with the piano accompaniment, the director of the college jazz program in my town is talking to my drummer and bass player. He sometimes wonders why he's spending his life training students in the jazz idiom. What future can there be in this music that no one cares about? It takes a lifetime to learn to play, and what of it then?

✳

Who Was Bill Evans?

Sister-in-law: "He seemed to absorb from William James the perplexity of never knowing things for certain. Even though there are no absolute answers and never will be, one has to act anyway."

Larry Bunker, drummer: "He sat sort of erect at the piano, and he'd start to play. And pretty soon his eyes would close, and his upper body would gradually start to lower itself, until finally his nose would be about an inch away from the keyboard. It was as if he were abandoning his body to his muse—as if the body evaporated, and there was some direct connection between his mind and the piano itself."

"Bill Evans? He was a punk."

✳

Scott LaFaro: A Fiction

The bass and piano were like two empty sleeves of a wool coat, filled by ghost arms.

The bass player and piano player were like two poles of a planet that through some magnetic accident grew closer and closer together until some new electric thing happened.

The implication of *one* is stronger than the taste of coffee, the smell of dead leaves in a rainy fall. Not *one* the number, not a person alone—that's a given in our lonely lives. Not *one* as in the first point in a list—top dog, lead dog, *numbah* one. But *one* as in the downbeat. That point in time that two or more jazz musicians (or classical players, blue grass pickers, rock stars, lounge lizards, studio cats)—must agree the start of the measure is. *One* is like the place the carpenter thumbs down the end of the tape measure. Measure twice and cut once, remember? Well, not in improvised music. In jazz you just eye it up and then slice that uncut diamond into the purest component of light.

How did Scott LaFaro know what not to play? They come to the band-stand in the dark basement club. Eisenhower is about to leave the scene, Ornette Coleman just on. LaFaro played around *one*. He played around the root—like loose soil, like the earthworm or the microbes taking waste to nutrient. The root is the foundation, the bass player's gig. Well, not only that, not after Scott LaFaro.

Can't we just tell you the end of the story and let you figure out what happened before you got here? Can't we skip all those transitions? Let go unsaid what everyone already understands? Scott LaFaro skipped ahead to the good parts, the musical dog-eared pages.

It's not like LaFaro can't walk. Ah, there's another jazz term with obvious metaphorical possibilities—the bassist playing those quarter notes in a line, four to a bar, setting the tension of the music in motion. LaFaro could play those quarter notes till the cows came. Till Houdini reappeared chain-free and breathing like a mortal.

He could swing hard. The multiple articulated note—playing C C C C C—the string of half notes where quarter notes would have been played by others, the suspension that delayed gratification, as in good sex—all those ways he could swing without obviously swinging. Abstract. Abstracted.

His phrasing is unexpected, the lines like so many boxcars, but then the strange uncoupling of melody from bar line. That's like holding hands with a goddess. It's implying things you don't need to say, if you can hear.

We don't need a photograph of that night that LaFaro must have sat in with Bill Evans the first time. We don't need to read about it.

He would push Evans: Man, you're fucking up the music. Cut out "the stuff," it's wrecking your life. And your playing. Don't give me this shit about transcendence and pain. Give me the space to play. I don't care if it's feeling or not, I don't care if it's a fucking sandwich.

To which Evans might have said, as he eventually did say, "Actually, I'm not interested in Zen that much, as a philosophy, or in joining any movements. I don't pretend to understand it. I just find it comforting. And very similar to jazz…. Like jazz, you can't explain it to anyone without losing the experience. That's why it bugs me when people try to analyze jazz as an intellectual theorem. It's not. It's feeling."

When Scott LaFaro died, in one of those car wrecks that killed more jazz musicians than dope ever did, Bill Evans must have gone into an odd-shaped room and never come out again except for food and water, and that only occasionally. He must have never played any note the way he would have played it otherwise. He must have taken no whole, real comfort in any good thing, not even music.

✳

Publishers' Weekly review, Bill Evans: How My Heart Sings, by Peter Pettinger

"Pettinger dispenses with personal insights to such a degree that his book becomes more critical discography than biography…. Intimates of Evans aren't described physically or characterized emotionally but are simply wrung dry of their musical content then pushed offstage. Interviews with contemporaries do provide memories of Evans, but they are often banal. In relating a life filled with romantic disappointment, extreme drug abuse and assorted illnesses that contributed to his early death in 1980, Pettinger paints only a pallid portrait of the man behind the music.

"In the end, fans of Evans's music may be left cold."

(Are we left so because Pettinger was himself a concert pianist and more interested in Evans' music than his life? Is that in turn because Evans' music was great and his life, however burdened by pathos, was just another life among the billions?

Is biography tyranny?

Who is any of us?)

✳

1. Fall 1973: Tells his long-time girlfriend Ellaine that he's leaving her, probably because she couldn't bear children, in order to marry a woman he's recently met. After he leaves for California and the woman he would marry, Ellaine throws herself in front of a subway train in New York. His manager arrives to identify the body.

2. July 6, 1961: Scott LaFaro, 25, bassist. Car accident.

3. Late 1971: Gary McFarland, 38, vibraphonist, collaborator. He, along with a friend, drank cocktails into which liquid methadone had been poured. Fatal heart attack. Both men died. Details remain unclear.

4. April 1979: Harry L. Evans, brother, schizophrenic. Self-inflicted gunshot.

5. September 15, 1980: Bill Evans, 50. Hepatitis. Liver failure. A life-time of drug use. Malnutrition.

6. August 23, 1998: Peter Pettinger, 42, pianist, Bill Evans biographer. Died just before his book on Evans was released.

7. "Every day you wake in pain like death."

8. "Many clubs pay more attention to their trash cans than the house piano."

＊

Larry Bunker, drummer: "I worked with him for a year and a half, and I really tried to get to know the man. And he would not have it....He'd sit and we'd hang, and pretty soon his eyes would glaze over. Then he'd take a paper napkin, draw a music staff on it, and start writing twelve tone rows—which, along with anagrams, was one of this favorite little mind recreations."

From an interview:

"Do you like people?"
"Yes, but I don't seem to communicate with them very well."

Is it important to communicate with people?"
"I dedicate my life to it."

"But sometimes in concerts or in clubs you fail to.... Does that disturb you?"

＊

December 31, 2012. My Interview With Bill Evans, In Which He Responds To My Question "Why Did You Behave The Way You Did Your Whole Life"?

what do you mean why what do you mean behave this suggests choice when we're busy making choices like what to play and what's going to happen next it's tempting then to look beyond what's true or might be

I don't know man I just didn't want to hang around that long and have everyone get tired there's beauty and then there's everything else and if you're interested in beauty then some of those day-to-day things eating sleeping keeping a schedule are going to fall away I'm not saying this is a good thing it worked for me though some people might say it hasn't

＊

Sometimes I wonder
what thoughts, what feelings he knew
as he was leaving.

Tell me what you remember
poor cold, silent autumn moon.

Kyogoku Tamekane (Sam Hamill, translator)

＊

My CD player has been fried, casualty of a power surge brought on by a faulty ballast in an ancient fluorescent light fixture in the basement. Or so the electrician said. I'm embarrassed that two months go by before I try to turn on the CD player and get nothing. How can two months go by where I'm not listening to anything but classical music on public radio? My router and modem were fried, too, and that I realized that within a few seconds. Given this, what is essential, according to me?

Perhaps turntables. With no working CD player in my home office now, I'm listening to vinyl for the first time in months or years. My LPs are mostly jazz albums I collected during college up until the advent of cassette, maybe ten years of penny pinching and used record stores, unearthing the occasional gem.

One of the only Bill Evans I have from those days is a rare reissue, "newly discovered tapes," that kind of thing, something I bought as late as '82 or '83: *California Here I Come*. Even Larry, my Bill Evans-worshipping piano player, has never heard of it. The title tune is hardly an Evans standard, but much of the rest of the double issue is mainstream Bill: "Polka Dots and Moonbeams," "Emily," "Very Early," "Stella by Starlight."

The recording pairs Bill with his *Kind of Blue* drummer, Philly Joe Jones (the one who, in the fifties, had introduced Evans to heroin).

I set the old turntable in motion. It starts spinning slowly and then builds up steam to about a standard 33 1/3. The first thing I hear is, of course, vinyl: its gray sound, its muted blues and shorn highs. I adjust the balance of the speakers, try boosting the bass, then the treble. I try getting more of everything.

I'm reminded how the first CDs sounded so cold to us: good for classical music, but definitely not right for jazz, I was not the only one to think.

Now vinyl is retro and back in style for millennials: its warmth, its evening of colors and articulation, its gauze or mesh over the midrange. But vinyl no longer sounds like real life to me—sun through clouds. So has real life changed or have I?

"Turn Out the Stars": Bill Evans' phrases are constructed to be broken into their logical and extra-logical parts. After the head, shards of melody lay across the canvas. We're told that a Bill Evans improvisation is a matter of ultimate preparation, music of the highest level, something he could turn on like a spigot. Maybe it's the left hand that seals the agreement with those who listen. No, if I single out the left hand, it means nothing without the theme and variation he plays in the right. Any given phrase he improvises is the logical sequel to the phrases before it, and leads to the phrase that follows. But perhaps that's true of any good player. And there is form over form, layer over layer: a descending line in one chorus picks up a simpler version of the same notes from the chorus before. Great tonal memory must be as keen as a dog's sense of smell.

Time is not a watch on a wrist. It's not "kept" by the bass or drums, like a secret lover in a garret, hidden away from the world. Time is malleable, gains and falls back like flowing water. But not so flowery as that. Time, the beat, is the cruel master. Some art is a piece of time carved out.

(If you're among the majority of people on the planet who don't listen to jazz and have never heard of Bill Evans, you could have skipped the preceding passage. But I decided not to tell you that until now.)

※

A True Story

"He once showed up for a gig with his right arm virtually useless. He had hit a nerve and temporarily disabled it while shooting heroin. He performed a full week's engagement at the Vanguard virtually one-handed, a morbid spectacle that drew other pianists to watch. He pulled it off, too, thanks in large measure to his virtuoso pedal technique. According to one bassist in the audience, 'if you looked away, you couldn't tell anything was wrong.' "

—VICTOR VERNEY

"You don't understand. It's like death and transfiguration. ...Each day becomes all of life in microcosm."

✻

Now what can I do?
My writing hand in a cast
is useless—
can't manipulate chopsticks
can't even wipe my ass!

Socho (translated by Sam Hamill)

✻

The Japanese

Nenette Evans: "He believed that there were many wonderful venues all over the world. I think above all he loved the Japanese audiences. Whenever a great piano was provided, he was normally ecstatic."

Bill Evans: "There is a Japanese visual art in which the artist is forced to be spontaneous. He must paint on a thin stretched parchment with a special brush and black water paint in such a way that an unnatural or interrupted stroke will destroy the line or break through the parchment. Erasures or changes are impossible...."

"The resulting pictures lack the complex composition and textures of ordinary painting, but it is said that those who see well find something captured that escapes explanation...."

✻

Lost

On September 16, 1980, I wrote a poem about Bill Evans and his influence on my musician friends and me. The poem began, "We said it always quickly like one word: billevans." The first line was perfect iambic pentameter, in a fourteen-line "free verse sonnet."

The poem went on to say that while other famous jazz artists were "Miles" or "Trane," billevans was always referred to by his full name—never "Evans" or "Bill." Then about line 9 of the poem, the trumpet player on a gig with me turns and asks me, "Hey, did you hear billevans died."

Though I've looked hard for it, I can't find a copy of my poem about billevans.

Later, I wrote another poem about billevans which I included in my second collection. Previously, I had tried to publish that poem in literary journals, but it was rejected fifteen times. I keep records of that; it reminds me of the lot of the jazz musician.

A gloss of that new billevans poem would say that it's better to fail beautifully than to succeed in a way that is basically untrue. Others might summarize the poem differently, however.

Of all my work, this poem is my piano player Larry's favorite poem. Of course, he never saw the poem that was lost. Almost no one did.

*

His Death

Coughing up blood, he complained of drowning. He lost consciousness in the car and his drummer carried him into the hospital.

*

Bill Evans: A Fiction in Monologue

It's the scale of everything that moves me the most in Japan, man. *(lights a cigarette)*. Little streets, little houses, little shops and restaurants with little plates of food in them. And then the plastic food labeled in the windows. All the cars there are white, did you know that? It's like, why would you want to step out of line to own something else?

The whole of the culture seems the opposite of spontaneous, and you don't lose face in front of your neighbor and your neighbor won't lose face in front of you. If you think of it, why not? Why shouldn't we each have our secrets, and within each secret is a thousand unknowns, and they're wrapped in nori and put on a plate: perfect presentation. What's really true, what's really felt, is so far within that it couldn't withstand the light of day. Even in a gray city. Tokyo. Yokohama. Dim lights in front of the club or off stage. Shards of light in the alleyway, the little streets, the little buildings. The scale.

※

On Audiences

"Some people just want to be hit over the head and, you know, if then they [get] hit hard enough maybe they'll feel something.... But some people want to get inside of something and discover, maybe, more richness. And I think it will always be the same; they're not going to be the great percentage of the people. A great percentage of the people don't want a challenge. They want something to be done to them.... But there'll always be maybe 15 percent ... that desire something more, and they'll search it out ... and that's where art is."

※

Visit the Bill Evans Archives

"Over 1000+ pages of materials, bound into four massive compendiums, now available by appointment. Handwritten music notation, lead sheets, personal letters & postcards, notes, art, scribblings, and more. Find out who the person behind the music really was, and why he made the choices he did, both musically and for his life.

"$100 Access for One Day"

※

Who Owns the Art?

In addition to Ken Burns' documentary and companion coffee table book ($45, available online for $14.78, used from $0.39, plus shipping.), the film-maker has released a series of audio recordings of jazz greats titled with his name first, followed by the name of the performer featured on that disc, *Ken Burns Jazz: Miles Davis. Ken Burns Jazz: Louis Armstrong*, and so on.

The compilation of these CDs is titled *Ken Burns Jazz: The Story of American Music*.

I guess we are to read the titles in the way we read Boswell's Johnson or Sandburg's Lincoln. I suspect, too, that the publishers rightly intuited that the words "Ken Burns" in the title would sell more copies than the word "jazz."

Jazz is a popular music that's not very popular. That much, in their research, the producers of *Ken Burns Jazz* had learned.

I once heard a panel discussion in which a group of documentary filmmakers complained about how much precious grant money Ken Burns has tied up.

Bill Evans never got a grant. There is no record that he ever applied for one.

✳

A True Story

My old friend the jazz pianist Lyle Mays tells a story something like this. He is a college student playing at a jazz festival in 1975 with a trio from North Texas State University—which is the Harvard of jazz, as anyone in the business knows. Guitarist Pat Metheny, already a professional, is also on the bill, and he and Mays meet at this venue and will hook up in a couple of years in a musical partnership that continued for decades.

One of the judges for the festival small group competition is Bill Evans. The panel of judges named Lyle's band Outstanding Combo at the festival. On his comment sheet on Lyle's playing, Evans had left the numerical scoring and written evaluation sections blank, and written instead only three words:

"See you around."

✳

On Audiences

"Sometimes we're really on and it doesn't feel like the people really understand what we're doing; other times, people applaud wildly after a tune when I didn't really think much was going on at all."

＊

Should anyone ever fail
this beautifully again,
promise me

your late conversion
won't keep you
from at least

sending word—that someone
hasn't once again
wasted life

on certainty.
Heroin, counterpoint,
Ravel, cocaine:

When he got into something
he really got into it.
It seems too much

to deny a man
slumped forehead to the keys
and their impossible jagged line

like black and white starlight,
his right arm limp with dead nerves,
while the left hand turns out the stars.

The shirt someone buttoned for him,
cigarettes on spring days,
the background chatter that wasn't there. Isn't.

How long it takes to die this way
when it rains outside, and within.
I suppose when the wind behaves,
the waves take note.

I'll hear that someone
came through the revolving door

again into
the shapeless dark
and began to play.

✳

Not long before his death Bill tried to reach Tony Bennett on the phone. They had made two recordings together when the singer was in the midst of his own drug problem and had lost his big studio recording contract.

Finally, after nights of trying to get through, Bill succeeded.

"Just keep going after beauty and truth," he told Bennett. "Forget everything else. Just beauty and truth." There was desperation in his voice. In weeks, he was dead.

Years before, he wrote a letter to his friend Gene Lees explaining that he started using heroin because he didn't think he deserved the fame and recognition that was his after playing with Miles Davis on *Kind of Blue*. "If people didn't believe I was a bum, I was determined to prove it."

✳

Nenette Evans, Letter to the Writer of This Account

"I think you understood some things about Bill that few other people did."

✳

His Two–Week Method of Learning Music

"Since there are only 12 notes in music, you can spend one day a week to learn everything there is about each note, and still take Sundays off."

✳

JFK would be 95. Bobby would be 86. Charlie Parker would be 92. John Belushi would be 63. Janis Joplin, 69. Sylvia Plath, 79. Miles Davis, 86.

Maybe we simply couldn't imagine them as elderly, as having trouble getting around, as not being ahead of where we are.

Scott LaFaro would be 78. Bill Evans would be 83. It's the jazz uber story. Car accidents. Narcotics. A life compressed. Among the jazz musicians who left life young, few were the picture of youth at the end of the years they had.

Or maybe everyone's got the whole thing wrong. Maybe what truth there was—that which preceded myth, anthologies, compilations, "desiccated biographies," commercial appropriations, neglect and deification, related tyrannies—maybe that bit of truth was lost like a scrap of paper filed away in a box. Maybe, all accounts to the contrary, Bill Evans' inner life was an act of tremendous ego, of supreme selfishness—first to sacrifice one's years practicing sixteen hours a day. Then at the end to close the door to the toilet and sit there in a cocaine haze. More than one critic notes that the fire and drive of his last quartet may have been due not as much to his being energized by youthful partners on bass and drums, as by his replacing heroin with cocaine as his drug of choice. From downer to upper. From cover it over to burn it down.

We'd like to imagine a truth more lyrical than any of these. We'd like to think we each could make something beautiful, something that might last, some one thing, some art. And think that someone who could make beautiful things again and again, each better than our best effort, that that person could not possibly be cognizant of his talent ("he lacked self-confidence.") To be aware of that gift would be like living in a body the entire surface of which was as sensitive as the fingertips, the genitals, the tongue. So hard and not worth it to be a genius, the rest of us have to think, and to be so driven and obsessed to use that genius, seeing so clearly that talent is nothing unless put into play, that life does not progress as much as it accretes moments. To see that one life among the billions, despite what the good-hearted say, cannot matter much. But music can. Sometimes.

※

Last Words to a Journalist Wanting to Ask More Questions in an Interview, Copenhagen 1980

"We have to run to catch a plane…. I have to go. Didn't you have a chance in all of that? I really have to go, I'm sorry."

✳

START here (again)

18. he never recorded country and western or contemporary Christian music

19. "I think he was out of his body when he played"

20. he wasn't an ascetic

21. Nenette Evans: "He hated electric guitars. He hated rock. Period"

22. in the 60s a record producer suggested he make a rock album

23. he was not a member of an organized religion, wasn't an activist in any political movement, nor a member of any fraternal society such as the Masons or the Rotary

24. in the middle of the night, Miles Davis would often call to go bowling

25. he could swing harder than some people gave him credit for

26. he was sometimes unaware of how his words and actions would be felt by those around him, including those close to him

27. he never performed at football, baseball, or soccer stadia

28. he said, "Ladies and gentlemen, I don't feel like playing tonight. Can you understand that?"

29. when he died, he was as old as he was going to get

30. he sometimes must have been aware how his words and actions would be felt by those around him

✳

"See you around."

Some Sources

How My Heart Sings, Peter Pettinger. *Kind of Blue: The Making of the Miles Davis Masterpiece*, Ashley Kahn. *Kind of Blue* liner notes, Bill Evans. *Turn Out the Stars* liner notes, Bob Blumenthal and Harold Danko. *The Best of Bill Evans Live* liner notes, Tim Nolan. "The Two Brothers as I Knew Them: Harry and Bill Evans," Pat Evans. "Bill Evans in Paris with Gene Lees," Steven Cerra. Review of *How My Heart Sings*, *Publisher's Weekly*. *Bill Evans Trio: The Oslo Concerts* (film). "On Ken Burns' Jazz Documentary and Bill Evans," Jan Stevens. "Bill Evans: Time Remembered," Jean-Louis Ginibre. *Stompin' at the Terrace Ballroom*, Philip Bryant. "Bill Evans" (poem), Richard Terrill. *The Essential Haiku*, edited by Robert Haas. "Artist Profiles: Bill Evans," Joel Simpson, allaboutjazz.com. *Meet Me at Jim & Andy's: Jazz Musicians and Their World*, Gene Lees. "Pianist Bill Evans and You, Professor," Jacques Berlinerblau. Bill Evans Archives (website). *Alone (Again)* liner notes, John L. Wasserman. "A Review of How My Heart Sings," Victor Verney, compulsivereader.com. "Interview with Nenette Evans," Jan Stevens, billevanswebpages.com. "It Was Just One Afternoon in a Jazz Club Forty Years Ago," Adam Gopnik, billevanswebpages.com. *All The Things You Are: The Life of Tony Bennett*, David Evanier.

Ozu's Tokyo Story (1953)

ORIKO IS THE FAITHFUL DAUGHTER-IN-LAW, WIDOWED BY WAR, never remarried, still in her prime. She is the only one who treats the parents with the respect due them in the culture—and she, as the father points out, not even a blood relative.

I open another beer. I think I've seen this one before, but I feel that about any film I see by Yasujiro Ozu: always the family, always people not saying what they think, unmoved through all the cruelty and pain. The same actors in every film. Sometimes, in the middle, especially late on a Friday night after a long week, I remember characters who aren't even in the story, but who were in the Ozu film I saw last weekend. The mother who abandoned the family will not reappear in act three because there is no mother, no one abandoned. Except maybe me, trying to make sense of things, so much enjoying being lost this way.

The scene in *Tokyo Story*, for instance, in which Kyoko, the youngest daughter, still living at home, berates her three elder siblings for having left too soon after their mother's death, her oldest sister already claiming some of the mother's clothes. "They're selfish," Kyoko says. "Even strangers would have been more considerate." Noriko, ever the conciliator, explains that when she was Kyoko's age, she too would have thought the sisters selfish. But in later years, a woman has a life apart from her parents. Children drift away. She must look after her own life.

Noriko tells the young Kyoko, "I may become like them, in spite of myself."

In this line resides the static, stoic, too-Japanese of Ozu. It's not even necessary to pay much attention to locate this sentiment. You can let your mind wander in and out, the way his camera never does. You can stream or borrow the film again next Friday (Critics rank Ozu among the handful of greatest filmmakers ever, but the Ozu disks are always on the library shelves.) You're going to confuse it with the other Ozu films you've seen anyway.

This time through the movie, not my first, I'm reminded of Douglas Sirk, the American director of those great fifties "weepies"—"women's films" such as the one where Rock Hudson goes to medical school so he can become a surgeon and restore Jane Wyman's eyesight, or the one where a faithful Black house servant is disowned by her ambitious daughter who tries to pass for White. Except that in Ozu, the Sirkian wash of gaudy primary color is replaced by stolid black and white. And except that there's a ton of feathers weighing down Ozu's camera's gaze. It never moves. Sirk's swirling melodrama is replaced by the Noh mask.

No, by the end of the film I think Ozu is like Sirk only in that they're both students of the family, perhaps the roots of all drama—the mostly unspoken, the under-demonstrated. And if family is impenetrable to any of us, the Japanese family, to the American audience, must be doubly so. Watching the family dynamic in Ozu is almost like watching the film without subtitles.

Kyoko, for instance, concludes the scene with Noriko by saying only, "I must get going," then heads off to her work. No reaction to Noriko's defense of the heartless older sisters; everything between the two women left implied.

"Goodbye, then," Noriko answers, and says no more.

I like watching movies from another time and culture, because even if the film is bad (and sometimes Ozu seems so), at least I'm learning something. It's like going on a very short trip and coming back. Or if the movie is cheap and commercial, at least it's commercialism designed to get money from people not me, from the pockets of some other era or population, and I can marvel how the audience then or there was hoodwinked by the facile and shallow and titillating—just as we are now by the latest Hollywood blockbuster or reality TV series.

I once was two hours into a two-hour-and-ten-minute Shohei Imamura film from the sixties before I realized it was supposed to be a comedy. Given my level of attention, you could argue I wasn't watching the film at all. But the images, the subtitled ambiguities, still gave pleasure—to be lost that way.

What wouldn't have occurred to me had I not sat down, too tired, to view the film?

At the end of *Tokyo Story*, for instance, if I hadn't heard Kyoko, the youngest daughter, half ask/half state, "Isn't life disappointing?"

Noriko, the widow, then smiles the unchanging smile of one who knows life is suffering, and that it's lived through its routine and its detail.

"Yes," she says. "It is."

Introduction to Film Section One, Tuesday 6-9:35 p.m., Fall Semester, 1996

I<small>T'S NOT UNTIL THE TENTH OR TWELFTH TIME</small> I <small>SAW</small> *T<small>OP</small> H<small>AT</small>* <small>THAT</small> I noticed how restless Fred Astaire looks at the beginning of the last musical number. He's acting more like a high school sophomore on a first date than the second highest box office draw of the 1930s (only Shirley Temple sold more tickets in those ten years.)

In this scene, Fred is seated on a park bench with Ginger Rogers. He rubs his left hand nervously on the top of his leg, as if he's trying to wipe something away. It's a movement without purpose, unlike the rest of Astaire, not part of some series of rhyming motions. His smile is static and unconvincing. The posture of this most graceful of movie stars is stiff and confined.

He's uncomfortable in his own body—how can that be? He looks away for a moment, to where we're supposed to think other couples are seated in this grand finale of the film. But on this twelfth viewing, I can't help but imagine a boom mike in his line of sight, or a key light about to blow. Or a nice-looking script girl—something outside the dream of the film narrative. Astaire can hardly wait to get up and dance, and that's the problem. Or he's worrying about the next scene, shot out of sequence, where he'll dance holding a priceless statue as his partner, or mow down metaphorical rivals for Ginger's hand using his gentlemen's cane as a machine gun.

After ninety minutes of formula courtship in *Top Hat*, the game is up, and Fred's won again. It's Ginger's turn to sing, and Fred now must be still and listen. It's hard for him, but this is the contract of the genre: first Fred sings and dances alone, then he sings to Ginger and she coyly takes a few steps that complement his. Then they dance "Cheek to Cheek," and in the second chorus of that Irving Berlin number he leads her to a ballroom set empty save for the two of them. There they dip to their graceful ritard. Boy meets girl, loses girl, and gets girl again—something like life. Or what audiences in the thirties, as now, wanted the movies to make them think life should be.

By the end of the third reel of *Top Hat* I know we'll be into the "The Piccolino," the big production number in which Irving Berlin sees how many ways he can rhyme the title: "Piccolino" and "go with your bambino," "where Latins sip their vino," "and we know," and so on. In 1936, this extravaganza may have been the reason people went to the film—their equivalent of today's car chase, intergalactic special effects, or exploding bodies in the apocalypse before the credits.

Sixty years later, the set full of dancers is fun for a minute or two, but every time the orchestra changes keys for another chorus of spins and twirls or overhead shots of couples making their Busby Berkeley kaleidoscope, I can hear the wooden seats in the auditorium creak. This is a four-hour night class, and Fred is not the only one restless. My students want to go home. Onscreen, groups of anonymous men and women, dressed to be multiple wedding-cake figures of Fred and Ginger, dance in circles. The women are on a kind of sash so that the men can cast them spinning away, but then reel them back in again like tired fish. Hardly a feminist statement. The choreography replicates that boy gets/loses/gets girl again narrative. Even my C students can recognize it, after I point it out, at least.

For this is English 114: Introduction to Film, at a provincial state university as far from Hollywood as the Depression was from the Italian Riviera in *Top Hat's* 1936. I am the teacher before the group of 230 mostly freshmen and sophomores, about 150 of whom show up on a given week. Maybe a dozen of those leave mid-film, and more leave during the production number, with half of the rest likely to leave at the break between the film and the lecture I'll present on it.

My job is to make them stay, to convince them that films which were popular a long time ago can tell us about who we are today. That the reason these genres—westerns, gangster films, musicals—have endured is…US. We're the reason that people in these films can walk down the street, fall suddenly in love, and stop in their tracks to begin to sing about it. They do so, I tell my students, because against all probability, we love it, just as the *Top Hat* audience did before their parents were born.

It's the same reason that so many students watch *Grease* for their extra credit paper on genre film. Remember, it's 1996, and *Moulin Rouge* is still five years away, *Chicago* is six, *Hamilton*, an infinity. About *Grease*, one student writes that she finds that "classic" movie to be as "fresh today as when it was made in the nineteen fifties." Others seem to agree. The problem, I write in the margins of her paper, is that *Grease* premiered in June of 1978—which means it became "classic" pretty quickly. Or more likely, I write, that "classic" now is a term borrowed from advertising rather than a marker of enduring value.

Maybe that's the basic question my class on (mostly old) movies is really asking—what endures? And why? And why such a question should be of import to people for whom time has been so short a string? For that student writer, for instance (who earned a B+) even *Grease* came out before she was born.

A further question I'm implying for them is, do you think people "then" were really so different from the way you are now? Like all the best questions, it's one to which I don't know the answer.

✳

I may have seen *Top Hat* twenty times by now, and I still sing along with the Irving Berlin tunes, secluded in my sound-proof projection booth. I still laugh at the minor characters—Blanche telling the boat captain to haul her husband off the deck where he sleeps on a pile of dead fish. "My Horace," Blanche tells him, "is the one with his mouth *closed*," and then a medium shot of Horace dozing in his formal wear amid the day's catch. I'm the only one in the present-day audience who laughs—my students not getting the joke on a single viewing, that the other dead fish are lying with their mouths *open*.

I love it when Horace's valet Bates encounters the local *cop Italiano*. Thinking the officer doesn't understand English, Bates enjoys piling on insult after insult. "You fish faced nincompoop, you mildewed donkey, you stultified shrimp." The cop answers *grazie* to each thrust, and then arrests Bates in perfect unaccented *Inglese* and hauls him off to jail. The scene is cut out of most of the prints the distributor sends to me, and most of the screenings I've seen on TV. I guess contemporary audiences don't appreciate the Depression era class warfare this scene presents—the oppressed manservant finally finding someone who he thinks is lower than himself, only to get busted. Americans long removed from the Great Depression are too busy denying that social class exists to understand the scene, which I admit seems a bit strained even to me. My students might argue, "Class warfare? Anyone can walk into a Wal-Mart." Or even "What do you mean, *class*?"

Humor is supposed to be based on surprise, the slip on the banana peel or the quick pie to the face, the snarky come back and rhythmic wordplay. So why do I laugh at these scenes each time through, and in fact laugh *more* the more familiar they become? Maybe it's the knowing laugh of the film nerd, the academic egg head—a laugh of appreciation, as if to say, "good show!" The truth is, because the films I choose are ones which I think do endure, I *like* having seen each of them six, eight, ten times. I no longer need worry about the protagonist's plight, no longer try to unsort the plot, or even to critique the acting, the score, the costume design. The film, the parts of it, exist for me now more like a painting, an *objet*. Through the repetition my job requires, I've stopped the motion in motion pictures. I've stopped time. Each time I see a great film, more of value is revealed to me.

But some of my 200 students feel that even one viewing of these old films is too many. They leave. Next week, to the students I can entice to stay in class after the movie, I'll argue that that week's film, *Dirty Dancing*, is really the same film as *Top Hat*. Spontaneous, rebellious, and fancy-free music man meets domesticating female counterpart who learns to dance ("learns to fuck"—I tell them without phrasing it quite that way, since that's part of the genre's code). In each case "Daddy" doesn't like it, but music and dance heal all; the unbridgeable gulf between the classes is closed.

Everything is all right at the end, as we knew it would be in the beginning. In *Dirty Dancing*, the costumes are different, but the pattern the same. What endures, indeed. The exams seem to indicate some of the students get the gist of it.

At first I was upset at the students' indifference, sometimes open hostility to what I was making them watch. These general education freshmen and sophomores (the weakest seem to be from the College of Education, for whatever that's worth) are so unlike the bright or at least earnest and polite English majors and grad students I get to teach in the rest of my professional life, where I pride myself on leading a good discussion and am confident about the results I get. Film, in contrast, is my "service course." Everyone in my department knows the class is suspect pedagogically—an English class with no discussion, no required writing assignments possible given the monstrous size. But we offer it nonetheless for a simple reason.

We need the money.

If we can enroll 200 students in a film class, and run three sections of the class, we've compensated for the money "lost" in a graduate seminar of only twelve. In my two sections of Intro to Film each year, I bring in more enrollment dollars than I would in three semesters of reasonably sized classes. In a private college or flagship State school, a class like this would employ four or five grad student assistants to lead discussion sections and give writing assignments. But to do so here would mean the class would cost my department more money than it makes.

Since I can't get to know many of the students, as I'd like to, the fun part of the assignment for me is getting to know these two-hour strips of celluloid each Tuesday night instead; the hard part is doing my best to teach the kids something. Which means first convincing them that what I have to say, what the films have to say, is important.

What do you suggest to improve this course? the course evaluation asks: "Show movies that are more popular." "Better Movies! Newer ones at least! (Bat Man, etc.)" "The Hitchcock films were boring!" "Ease up a little and make the course more fun. Isn't 'science fiction' (Star Trek) or 'action films' (Rambo) important too?"

The cruelest responses are the ones that I most remember, and I confess they sometimes make me laugh, like this one, scrawled in a nearly unreadable hand:

"Try watching movies that do not suck shit. Some were o.k. others were so boring that I didn't want to be here (so I left"

And this bit of advice from another displeased student, most telling of all: "He should show the films that WE like not the ones HE likes."

Students in my lit and writing classes are less likely to offer an opinion on which texts to study. But film is a commercial medium. Everyone is entitled to an opinion on each film, and in fact is encouraged to have one, since those with more opinions will be those who buy more tickets to feed the corporate fantasy machine. How bewildering to students to suggest that there are ways to assess the value of a film beyond what one does or doesn't like. Before this semester, it's all they've ever been asked.

✳

On any given Tuesday, my job is also to run the projector.

Example: Reel one of *Citizen Kane* ends with Charles Foster Kane signing his "Declaration of Principles," which he will post as an editorial on the front page of his newspaper the first day he's in charge. In the Declaration, the millionaire Kane pledges to fight for the working man (that class that so few of my 1990s students know that they belong to) and print the news for him straight. Jed Leland, Kane's partner in crime from college days and soon to be drama critic for the newspaper, says in a close up, "I'd like to keep that particular piece of paper myself. I have a hunch it might turn out to be something pretty important... like the Declaration of Independence, or the Constitution..." (I can recognize, after repeated viewings, that this speech foretells Charles Foster Kane's later fall, as he doesn't keep his pledge.) Then we get a close up of Leland himself, the beautiful face of the young Joseph Cotten as he adds, "...and my first report card at school."

At that point I'm poised and ready. I see the white dot in the upper righthand corner of the screen, and then the second white dot—my cue. I have already released the clips holding film reels onto the projector. When

Leland finishes the line about his report card, I turn off the projector, spin the leader onto the take up reel, and ease the full take up reel off the back sprocket. I quickly shift the empty reel to the back and slide the full second reel onto the front. I thread the leader snake-like through the projector and out the back. I attach the leader to the back reel, then spin it forward by hand past the "8-7-6-5" numbers, which I can see because I hold my pocket flashlight up to the film. Then I pass the blank frames, just to the point that I see the images begin.

I turn the control knob to "project bright" and movie time begins again. Real time elapsed: about 15 seconds!

Since I'm not a projectionist by trade, I take pride in completing this regimen. In movie theaters, since long before 1996, films came in giant boxes—two or three reels-worth rolled onto one—so that projectionists could flip a switch at the beginning, then leave to go sell popcorn or step out for a smoke. Even in the older days of multiple reels, theaters had a two-projector system. When the first white dot appeared in the corner of the frame, it was the cue for the projectionist to start the second projector, screen time flowing seamlessly from one magic lantern to the next, something like passing a baton in a relay race.

My first semester teaching Introduction to Film, I tried the two-projector method, and I could make the story pass from one runner to the next without dropping the baton. Sometimes the second runner had to slow down a bit to wait for the first. But not bad for an English teacher.

Soon I gave up on trying to make time flow between the two projectors. The problem was that I had only one *good* projector, which the English Department kept locked in a cabinet, so faculty from other departments couldn't use it and wear it out. There were a bunch of other projectors lined up on the counter for general use, the way old cars are lined up in salvage yards, in their varying degrees of rust. These antique projectors were all Bell & Howell—a company that stopped making movie projectors in the early 1970s. Now, after a merger, they specialize in financial services.

I wonder how many of my students suspected that there was something wrong with a system that had them pay tuition to sit before this level of technology. Perhaps the world did not think them as important as their parents worked to convince them they were. And for that I am sorry and a little ashamed. Each week, every semester, when the screen went dark between reels, the students' collective groan was the same. A few students would look back to watch me work in the projection booth, and I felt for those fifteen odd seconds as much performer as prof.

Over the years, I found that other reels in other films end at inopportune times. There is the break between reels two and reel three of Spike Lee's *Do the Right Thing* that comes right in the middle of the riot sequence, after Mookie has thrown a garbage can through the window of the pizzeria, but before Ruby Dee screams "Nooo, Nooo," as she watches the neighborhood burn. Hitchcock's *North by Northwest* runs well over two hours, so there's a fourth reel to the film. My students had been conditioned to sit through two blackouts, and that third gap of silent darkness, and the continuation of the chase scene—on Mt. Rushmore in the dark, no less—onto the fourth reel they found too much to bear. Sometimes, despite my nimble hands, they simply left.

I'd learned to control what transpired in that projection booth. I'd learned the content of each film, image by image. But the all too human reaction of the young people in my charge remained beyond my control.

✳

1996: The auditorium for English 114 holds creaky wooden seats that test the severity of angles young backs can assume. The sound system in the auditorium yields muffled dialogue and wavering music. On older prints with ragged soundtracks, the sound lacks depth, like the voices that announce flight times in airports. When I show *Cabaret* each term, I have a choice between blasting the dance production numbers at earsplitting levels or asking the students to read lips during the intimate scenes between Liza Minnelli and her beau. I've dumped a whole unit on film noir because, shot in high contrast deep shadow as the genre dictates, the stories on my projector were rendered in total darkness.

Other problems coexist. A hand-lettered sign posted on each door of the room reads: WARNING: THIS AUDITORIUM IS NOT AIR

CONDITIONED." No shit, I think. The room is packed with young bodies every Tuesday night. During one September heat wave, I recorded the
room's all time high: 88 degrees. Surely this is against some law, but one that
doesn't apply to students at small public universities.

These students are packed in the room not because I am so popular
a teacher, but because among the classes that satisfy a general education
requirement, Introduction to Film is the only one for which students know
they won't have to read books and write papers. It's not possible, not in the
budget. Instead, I give long multiple-choice exams that I hope will test the
content of the class rather than a student's skill at taking tests.

For all these reasons, for five or six years I beg off from teaching Intro
to Film, resign myself to doing the extra work that another writing or reading class requires of me instead. But then I decide to give Intro to Film
another try. The auditorium has been refurbished with a new projection
system and the modern equivalent of Sensurround that makes the audience feel like they're in the best seats in a concert hall. There are plush new
seats for the students, and a podium of high-tech toys for the teacher that
someone my age must relearn each semester after the latest upgrade. DVDs
have made it cheap to show anything, and Blue Ray has made it beautiful. I
feel like Captain Kirk on the bridge: press a button and the clip I've book-
marked, or the interview with the director or the eminent critic, appears
magically onscreen. I'm as much the conjurer as George Méliès, that silent
film pioneer I show in week one, who made moon men disappear with a
puff of dry ice smoke, simply by stopping the camera, removing one actor,
freezing the rest of the cast in place, and then cranking the camera once
again. Something like me in that old projection booth, Méliès could stop
time.

And further miracles: Air conditioning so effective that students are
chilled awake through even the "boring-est, suckiest, most disgusting movies" I can find. But the greatest gift of all: ironically, the class is now less than
half the size it was, because the weakest students can now fulfill their Gen
Ed requirement with a new class in the music department: The History of
Rock and Roll.

Even more than English, the long-suffering music department needs the money.

The students who are left to me, though still most interested in their grades and getting out of class on time, are actually interested in films. A few tell me they'd like to work in Hollywood; some have made their own films they'd like to show me. The rest are at least open to the possibility that audiences for those "classic" films faced some of the same worries, felt some of the same conflicts as they do, and that the films will render those worries and conflicts on screen. They might become convinced that a film's value, as with that of any work of art, can be appraised by looking closely at its constituent parts. The assessment of that value can never be purely objective, since the film's goal is to make us think something and, mostly, to make us feel something. But we can nevertheless try to make that assessment, and some films will endure.

My class evaluations skyrocket. I pretend in reports to the Dean that this is due to my advanced age and experience.

But I realize now that the films I saw each term had become more real for me than the students for whom I screened them. I'm not proud of this, but it's true. How could it not be true, given that I saw each student as one among many over a single semester, but I saw each film again and again? Who, I think now, were all those farm and suburban kids in those creaky wooden seats in that large and airless room back in the early nineties? What were they doing here, and what did they want from me? Who were these naive Hollywood wannabes in the later years?

The films for me were far more nuanced. They had ceased to be merely narratives. They had become the succession—and the repetition—of their lines and images. The images followed one another in the dark; the weeks of showings followed one another on the screen I lowered at the start of class in the giant room.

✳

If it's '96, I'm in my projection booth, reading lips on the screen, doing the dialogue myself between bites of microwaved dinner. Some lines I can deliver with perfect pace and inflection. Nicholson to Polanski in *Chinatown*: "I like my nose... I like breathing through it." Dietrich to Welles in *Touch of Evil*: "I didn't recognize you. You need to lay off those candy bars." John Wayne's Ethan Edwards in *The Searchers*: "We'll find 'em all right....as sure as the ... turnin' of the earth."

Subplots in the films have become wonderfully clearer: the implied love affair between Ethan and his brother's wife in some distant past of *The Searchers* becomes as obvious as if it were printed in a subtitle, the way operas in Italian are titled in English above the stage. There are the gaffs I catch in repeated screenings: the power lines visible in the distance in that last crane shot of *High Noon*. In *Stagecoach*, how the shadow of the camera is visible as the horses pull the rig into a swollen river.

And my interpretation of the films has grown as well. I used to think that Jed Leland's picture of Charles Foster Kane—"Charlie never gave anybody anything," he should "go to Africa and lord it over the monkeys"—was clearly the correct one. Seeing the film for the tenth or twelfth time, I began to see that Leland's view of Kane was as flawed as anyone's. Jed Leland really was a "stuffed shirt," a "New England schoolmarm," as Kane thought him. I had merely understood Leland's view of Kane the most clearly because I was nearly as cynical a man as Leland. Or maybe because Joseph Cotten's performance is so attractive. Great art in any form not only endures. It seems to change as we change. You can't sit in the same aisle seat twice.

And there's perhaps my favorite line of all. It's in the French experimental short film *La Jetée*, in which a man is sent from the post-nuclear future back to the past, our present day, in order to change history. It's his own attempt to manipulate time, and it almost succeeds, until we learn that the murder on an airport jetty that he had witnessed as a boy, that had haunted him for years, was his own.

My favorite line has nothing to do with that ironic ending. It describes the Paris rebuilt after The Bomb, devoid of beauty and everything that made it the city it had been. Paris has become, to some unidentified narrator, "a million incomprehensible avenues."

I like that. It says something about the folly of human progress, about the inevitable apocalypse those Frenchmen thought we were condemned to in 1962, when *La Jetée* was made. It says something about the fear the future should hold for us, which is why, perhaps, we've been made to live one day, one life at a time. A million incomprehensible...somethings.

The most compelling questions are the ones that remain unanswered. Call it "general education."

*

In that class back in '96, the third reel might have fluttered at its bitter end in *Kane* or *The Public Enemy*. I might have had to turn the projector off and on more than once to get the sound ironed into recognizable speech. I could then walk out of the booth to check the volume, maybe bump it up a notch. Sharpen the focus. What control I had! Then I would put out the little light in the booth and sit back in my chair isolated from the real world. A master of miracles and these machines. I had made time stop and started it again, with only a minor jolt to the galaxy. And after 120 minutes, plus lecture time, I'd go home singing "Cheek to Cheek," or reciting Jimmy Stewart's filibuster speech on the Senate floor in *Mr. Smith Goes to Washington*, or feeling moved at how *Rear Window* captures the angst of the peeping Tom.

Maybe when I got home, there would be a ballgame on TV, something I didn't know the outcome of. I knew there was beer in the ice box. There would be this other leap in time, between the end of the film and the taking up of my life. My walk home through real darkness, past the box-like buildings of the campus, the beginning of the residential neighborhoods, slight of traffic, no one on the street. There would be the lights of my family in our three-bedroom rambler, across the park and down the cul de sac, six tenths of a mile from Wiecking Auditorium. It would be as if none of the rest ever happened at all. As if it would never happen again, not until the beginning of next semester.

III

Postscripts to
Late Middle Age

NEIGHBORS ════════════════════

"BY THE WAY," I ADD, "THANKS FOR KEEPING YOUR DOG QUIET EARLY in the morning. Jerry told me he'd talked to you."

"It's not my dog that's barking," the neighbor woman answers. She's short and round in her neat shorts and flowered top; permed, mouse-brown hair. A gaggle of children are playing in her front yard, two hers, the rest her day care. I see and hear their parents drive in and out of her drive-way each day before eight and again after five, an action which sets the dog off into loud spasms.

"It's the dogs behind me on Duluth Street that are barking so early."

"Well, we appreciate it anyway," I say about what I'm implying should be her efforts to keep her dog in line.

I find it hard to like or even respect this neighbor woman very much, and I'm not sure why. I'm not proud of the fact I don't like her, but some-times, to myself, I call her "Mrs. Mom" or even "Baby Factory." Her husband I call "Soldier Boy"—just to myself, not even to my wife and certainly not to other neighbors. And about the time I start feeling guilty for my epithets and hasty generalizations, their dog starts in again—they must not even hear it. "Baby Factory," I whisper alone in my kitchen.

Jerry lives next door to Heather, and their two houses are directly across the street from mine. We're new in the neighborhood—two years—and Heather, James, and clan moved in just before we did. Soldier Boy (James) has been away for months, called up with the reserves to go fight in Iraq—actually to load airplanes in Saudi Arabia, Jerry tells me. I didn't even notice he was gone. Soldier Boy is not a boy, and not even a full-time soldier. He manages a finance company in the next suburb, Jerry says. I'm not one to socialize with the neighbors, and don't care what they do at their house, as long as I don't have to hear it. I like quiet. But Jerry tells me everything. Jerry is one of the many original homeowners on our pleasant, tree-lined, block-long street in our predictable suburb. The houses were built mid-sixties. From all appearances, this is a nice place to live.

The day we moved in was the hottest of the summer two years ago. It was the day in which, in the town we moved from, a professional football player died from the heat at a summer practice (I think the widow settled out of court.) Even as the movers, two skinny guys, were lugging our furniture into our new house, Jerry came over to my door to introduce himself. Linda and I were trying to direct the movers as to what went where. Jerry began to tell us about Neighborhood Watch, the annual meeting, the previous owners of our house, and more. "Excuse me," the movers said to him, straining on either side of the couch they were carrying. Jerry was planted right in front of our door and they couldn't get around him.

"Jerry doesn't appear to know about boundaries," Linda offered that first evening. "He's probably not a bad guy, but I wonder about his people skills."

I suggested that it's best to keep a distance from all the neighbors.

※

The offending dog is a rust-colored retriever, the quintessential family dog—big, dumb, and friendly. The neighbor couple contains Maggie's exuberance with one of those invisible fence arrangements in the front of their yard. It's a perfect metaphor for suburbia, it occurs to me: an unmarked border that one can choose to stray beyond only at the risk of a jolt of pain.

Our master bedroom juts out toward the street, toward our across-the-street neighbors, in our L-shaped rambler. When anyone walks in or out our front door, Maggie, bound by her unseen master, launches into a fit of barking. When anyone goes down the street—a jogger putting in her daily paces, a kid on a scooter or bike—Maggie marks her place in the world in her sharp red voice. When the wind blows the treetops in a way suspicious to her. When a squirrel runs across the lawn two houses away. When something occurs to the red doggie mind that deserves a response, the barking starts, intermittent yet inevitable, so that the listener can divide time into that being filled by noise and that which is only the period between episodes. These are not good moments. On an oscilloscope, the bark would have sharp peaks, like geologically youthful mountains. It's jagged like a nerve under a pitchfork. I've found I can hear it even from my back yard.

Sometimes the dog's owners are not around when the noise breaks off a piece of day from the neighborhood. One time, getting out of my car, my dark side responds to the dog. "Shut up," I say. Bark. "Shut up," I say louder. Bark. "Shut up!" Bark. Each time I speak more directly to the animal. Which of us is more single-minded?

Just then, Heather appears at the front door—she was home this time after all, and gives me a look that even at this distance seems to say this is my problem. She calls the dog inside. "What's wrong with her?" I think. "What's wrong with him?" her look says she's thinking.

I don't mind dogs, really I don't; it's dog owners whose failings are only too obvious.

Another time I'm going to get my mail. Our box is across the street from my place and at the foot of Maggie the retriever's driveway. The woman and the kids are on the front lawn. The children, preschool age, are surprisingly pleasant, despite their need for attention. "Tomorrow I'll be six!" one cries to me, a perfect stranger. Then Maggie starts with her romp and bark, back-pedaling, threatened at my approach. This time I'll take a different tack, I decide. I walk inside the invisible line that holds her, bend at the waist and knees and hold out one hand, make a smooching sound with my lips. The dog bounds back and away up the driveway, stops barking for a moment, then hunches into her back legs and pisses onto the blacktop. A sign of greeting, I know, but not the most charming one.

"I just can't make friends with her," I say. Heather agrees, maybe too quickly.

Jerry has talked to me about the dogs in the neighborhood. He's up early every day (he's a retired engineer—restless, too much time on his hands, I think), so the barking doesn't bother him. But Wilma, his wife, likes to sleep in until eight a.m. "The barking begins at 7:15," he says.

"Every day, bar none," I agree.

"It's not neighborly," he says. "And," he lowers his voice even though we're talking on the deserted suburban street in front of his house. "It's against the rules of New Brookside." The guy behind him has a dog, and next to that two dogs, Jerry says, and one starts barking early, and then Maggie starts in with her barking and then the first answers back. People are trying to sleep. People want quiet.

Jerry isn't a bad guy, I think.

Jerry asked Heather to keep the dog quiet early in the morning. "She got a little defensive," he tells me. "They're great neighbors," (I'm wondering why he thinks so), "and you hate to complain," Jerry says. "Eventually it leads to bad relations."

It seems to me that the bad relations have already begun.

"If you see her out, you might back me up a little, thank her for keeping the dog quiet."

I say I'll do that.

At the National Night Out neighborhood meeting last summer—Jerry, of course, is block captain—for the entertainment of the group Jerry pull-started an antique gasoline jack hammer on which he had emblazoned a hand lettered sign reading, "Knock the Heck Out of Crime." On Memorial Day morning (not early, he's not a hypocrite) he stood in front of his flag-pole and blew taps on his bugle. He'd told me a few days before what he was planning to do to mark the holiday, and I'd laughed because I thought he was kidding. But then that Monday, Jerry stood ram straight while his faded American flag fluttered in the spring wind. I admit I counted the stars to see if there were fifty. And I thought of the bugler playing the solemn taps at JFK's funeral, a marking point of my childhood. But unlike that musician, Jerry didn't miss a note.

✳

It's 2003. Our country is at war, the president tells me. It's a war, and we're winning, don't worry, though he is certain the war will last a long time. In the end, if we don't give up, we'll win. We have to be vigilant to protect our security.

God is on our side, and we're fighting for truth and peace, against evildoers. Now that we've defeated our enemy in Iraq, the world is a more peaceful place, even though there's still a war there.

I'm writing a letter to the future and in it I ask if we're still around. Is the war over, I ask? Is it ever? Are we the people we were before my day took us into this war, or have we always been this country that I have come not to recognize? Has it been twenty years that this America has been on this long slide toward ... toward what? Permission we grant ourselves to look the other way? A notion that we need not see beyond our neighborhoods? Beyond our sacrosanct "families"? Invisible fence.

Time travel would allow me to see my day in the light shed from another time. Are we gonna make it? Or have we just always been this way—bullying, arrogant, disturbing the peace—and I'm only now coming to see it?

In my letter, I tell the future about my other neighbor Robert, a retired shop worker, the one person on the block who I know is a Democrat, besides Linda and me. "The last few years, 2003 and 2004, living in the United States," he says, "I feel like I'm in the middle of a Nazi party rally." In my letter I say that I agree.

I write how, in one of his sincere but ill-timed visits, Jerry tells me that James is coming home from the war, and to mark the event, Jerry will purchase small American flags that he is going to put on every lawn in the block as a welcome home gesture.

Jerry means well, and often does well. James has been away from home and now he's coming home again. I see that. But I tell Jerry we don't agree with the war so we can't go along with the plastic flag in our lawn. We have nothing against James personally (it's his dog I dislike, but I don't say that.)

Then Jerry says yes, but James is serving his country.

And I nod, but I think a lot of people who aren't in the army are also serving their country, but I don't say that either and merely hope Jerry has made note of our wishes to be left out of the patriotic display.

Nothing happens for a few days, almost a week, and I think the plan has changed. Then on July 3, I awaken to see a small American flag at the foot of our driveway, a symbol repeated at the foot of every drive on our block.

I don't say anything about it to Linda, since I know she'd be more upset even than I am.

Or should I not be? Is this merely a generic gesture for the Fourth of July? Or is James coming home this weekend, coincidentally on the holiday? "Flying the flag doesn't mean what it used to mean," neighbor Robert tells me. "We think we have the right to invade any country, whether or not innocent people will be killed.

"They talk about deaths in America. Don't other people's lives count? And now that we've started this war, Americans shouldn't question it, or they're seen as unpatriotic."

"They're seen as unneighborly," I agree.

"Yeah, lots of flags. Like Munich, Berlin," Robert says. "I was in the service, too, once..." He's leaning on his garden rake, well into the speech he knows I'll agree with. I'm a safe audience and a good neighbor, and want to be.

"Laws and rights in the Constitution can be suspended by the government any time they feel like it. And the people are supposed to just roll over and shut up. It's like a different country."

The symbol of this different America here on Hansen Avenue in New Brookside? A plastic stick and sheet of polyester, printed and made in China, total one foot in height now planted in my lawn.

How to celebrate now, and what? Are our enemies, no matter how horrible their deeds, cast into the position of right because of the unequaled power of their foe? Seeing that smaller version of the same flag that flies proudly above Perkins and Wal Mart and Bob's Slightly Used Cars, I ask myself that oldest of suburban questions: What will the neighbors think? What will they think I mean by having a flag in my lawn right now?

For the first day I do nothing. That night I talk to Linda. She wants the flag gone. Jerry, I'm convinced, did not even hear my telling him not to do his Iwo Jima trip on our property. But if I am to take it down, how am I to go about it? Pick it like a dandelion? Transplant it in the lawn next to his twelve-inch plastic flag, without comment? Put it between his doors with a note: "Displaying this flag at this particular cultural moment is making a political statement with which I don't agree; what's more, displaying it in my lawn against my wishes is contrary to the principles for which I think this flag should be a symbol, but currently is not."

Or should the note read, "Jerry, sorry," and leave it, politely, at that?

Maybe we should we burn the flag, do it in the street in front of the neighbors' houses. But since people in the burb seldom leave their houses, the bonfire wouldn't make much of a statement. Maybe we need to torch the whole neighborhood, to destroy the suburb in order to save it.

In any event, do we want to be the only one on the block without the flag in front of our house? I notice that Robert, as riled up as he is about the war, has not taken the trouble to object about the flag at the foot of his driveway. Should we do nothing and bend to the will of the majority? Do I want to alienate my neighbor Jerry, who is surely well meaning, as I said, and who is my ally against Soldier Boy and Mrs. Mom's dog? Do I want to get Solider Boy mad at me, given that Jerry and I might need some of his good will in the dog situation? Do I want "bad relations"?

What's more important, that I act consistent with my beliefs, or that we not piss people off for no big reason, when the result of their anger might be years of hearing their G.D. dog bark, and no further recourse?

I notice on the very day Jerry has planted the flag, a young man walking his own dog down our street. I see his eyes move from house to house, seeing the uniformity of the flags. I imagine he thinks the way I think, and sees the display as appropriate to one of those Party rallies in Munich that Robert is talking about. The young man feels alienated, like he's not at home in his own country. Or being young and impressionable, he's encouraged by the display not to question the war. If the entire block of Hansen Avenue feels this way, surely it must be so.

It's also true that not many people walk down our block-long street. I ask our adult son, who's living with us this year, what he would do about Jerry and the flag. He answers that to him it doesn't make that much difference (the watchwords of his generation), but he knows it pisses us off more than it does him.

Later that day I'm driving through New Brookside. Flags are everywhere. I count the number of seconds I can drive down the arterial road near our house without being in sight of some kind of flag or patriotic display. I never can count past four-Mississippi.

I notice this day too that Heather has put a yard sign up, "Liberate Iraq: Support Our Troops" (Letter to the Future: these signs are everywhere now, ten to one outnumbering the signs that read, "Support Our Troops, Bring Them Home" or "Say No to Permanent War." I imagine everyone will forget this soon, so that's why I'm telling you now.)

Stamped on Heather's Iraq sign, at an angle as if by some oversized Pentagon bureaucrat, is the annotation in all caps, MISSION ACCOMPLISHED. Just today a nineteen-year-old boy from a nearby suburb was killed in Iraq. There is anarchy throughout that country we've invaded. The country's national museum has been looted. There is no police force, no government, no public services, no medical care. Just what mission has been accomplished? I guess it's the mission of having one husband and father about to come home safe. A youngish woman alone in a rambling house in the suburbs surrounded by her small children and day care charges, an unruly dog—I can't question her motives, even if the message that results from them is abhorrent to me.

But is the flag in my lawn saying I agree with her surmisal?

"Look," I propose to Linda, "it's Fourth of July weekend. Flying the flag then is not quite so bad as otherwise." I say this, but deep down don't believe it. "Jerry just simply didn't hear me tell him to leave us out of the display. He expects conformity. If the flag is still there Monday morning, I'll take it down. I won't allow him to put it back up when Soldier Boy comes marching home in one of his SUVs."

By Sunday afternoon, Jerry has taken down the flags. So I conclude it was a holiday celebration. End of story.

But I noticed that Heather had a number of relatives over at her house on Saturday for an All-American barbecue. I didn't hear her damn dog, so it was a nice day. The weather was very hot and humid (almost like the day we moved in) so we had the air conditioner on and the windows closed. The quiet, though artificial, was welcome. I repeat to myself that I don't care much what the neighbors do or say out of my earshot, flags or not.

Then by mid-week I see a large man around Heather's house (there are often men coming and going—her day care parents, and her brother, so Jerry tells me, who is helping out in James's absence.) But this large man is taking golf clubs out of one of the several oversized SUVs that always seem to be parked in the driveway. I notice that the yellow ribbon that Heather had tied around the ash tree in the front yard is gone. The candle in the window is no longer burning nights. Soldier Boy is home, and the flag in my yard was there for him, and I didn't even know it. Whatever statement I was making or not, it's been made. Mission accomplished.

Once Soldier Boy returns, I never again hear Maggie's voice in the early mornings.

✳

At any given moment, I don't know much. But I know I don't know much, and although I don't like thinking this way, increasingly it seems that other people aren't as aware of their own ignorance as I am of mine. I witness people around me, and not just younger people, doing things that I know for sure are silly: running up credit card debt, supporting a made-up war, and letting their dogs bark endlessly and not giving a second thought to any of it. I don't say anything to these people about their actions any more than I go up and call them to their faces, "Soldier Boy" and "Baby Factory."

In contrast, when I was younger, I was more likely to say something to people whose thinking I thought was in error. But I was less likely to be able to recognize the error.

I'm bothered by my own formulations. One bad thing about being on the political left is the plethora of meetings and committees to address problems that could be solved more easily if we just threw money at them. Another bad thing about being on the left is that by definition we're plagued by doubt. Those on the right have their moral certainty, their belief that life is essentially simple; those on the left hold to a relativity of values, believe that life is rich in proportion to its complexity. Thus to grow old and more sure of more things and remain a liberal is no small feat.

Here's one point I am becoming more sure of: There is a direct connection between what goes on in my suburb and what goes on in the world outside of it. There's a connection between barking dogs and aggressive foreign policy, between silent, nasty name-calling of neighbors you wish would move and the decline of civility in our public discourse. A connection between our flying the flag of *my family* and our lack of concern for others beyond that immediate family.

Here's one point I'm not sure of: what are those connections?

✳

It's summer, a Saturday. I pull into a Super America in a nearby burb, top off the tank of my Subaru, doing my part for global warming, and am about to drive away when around the corner strides a line of children, one fiftyish woman in their midst. I think to myself, "I've never seen so many kids in my life." One small kid pushes a stroller, and a couple of bigger ones are only a few steps ahead. I notice too that they all look alike, but then think it can't be; some must be neighbor kids. This chain of thoughts occurs in about two seconds, something less than a moment. I count nine children in all.

"I know," the fiftyish woman calls to me, a perfect stranger, from near the door to the gas station. Her hair is thin and a ragged orange. She's dressed in a plain smock. "I know what you're thinking: You've never seen so many kids in your life."

It's uncanny. I feel like I've stolen something and been caught.

"That's right," I reply. I'm trying to sound upbeat, which is not my long suit.

Her tone rises slightly. "And thanks to God for the life of every one of them!" She pauses. "And yours, too."

Not long after, on another summer day, I run across the street to likable Jerry's place to loan him a piece of computer software he asked if he could borrow. Once inside, I'm greeted by Jerry and Wilma wearing long faces. "Did you see this morning's *Post*?" Jerry asks.

The headline reads, "Son Arrested in Death of New Brookside Man."

The man living two houses down from Jerry, the house next to the one with the barking dog, was killed by his own son the previous morning at the son's house in the suburb one over from ours, the one that had the gas station I patronized. Jack the deceased was 66, and his wife, also attacked by the son, was in stable condition. It was strange to recognize in the newspaper article house numbers so close to my own address on our block long street. "The suspect had previously lived with his parents in the 6400 block of Hansen Avenue in New Brookside."

The article also says that "Investigators were seen putting a hammer into an evidence bag." It ends with a testimonial from Jerry himself, a long-time neighbor, reacting to the event with the shock that one would expect to hear on a tree-lined street in a suburb far from death.

"'Jack and Yvonne were wonderful neighbors,' said Jerry Clark, leader of the neighborhood watch club. 'They often walked the street, and attended nearby St. Joseph's Catholic Church.'"

I agree with Jerry that they were good neighbors, since I never knew they were there. I often saw the victim outside working on his lawn, and once or twice I may have waved. Linda and I admired his beautiful brick driveway on our own jaunts around the neighborhood. That was about it.

Back at home I share the gruesome news with Linda and together we read the rest of the article:

"'Jack Kingsley kept his yard groomed and had the driveway rebuilt with inlaid brick,' neighbor Jerry Clark said. He noted that a few years ago Kingsley narrowly escaped death after his canoe tipped while he was fishing on Lake Independence early in the year. Kingsley managed to swim to shore with his life jacket and made it to a business where he warmed up."

Linda and I agree that we never met the man.

✳

It's spring of the following year. America's war goes on, and occasionally Robert and I complain and worry on nice afternoons in my yard or in his. Jack Kingsley's house has been spruced up and we expect it will go on the market soon. Baby Factory is pregnant again—with number three, and one suspects they're not through by a long shot. James has gone to and returned from the Middle East once or twice more, Jerry has told me. Maggie the

Retriever has been decidedly quiet. I wonder what the relationship is among several of these developments. Has the neighbor couple heard my complaints? Unlikely. Did Jerry prevail on them that Wilma needed her sleep? Or does James' presence in the household, as I suspected, make it easier to keep the dog in check?

I have professed not to care about what goes on in my neighborhood as long as it doesn't bother me. I always assumed the whole world was my neighborhood and to become too engrossed with the local is simply to not be a good citizen and maybe not even a good person.

But in my own way, I'm becoming very involved with the neighbors, if noticing them is such a beginning. I've noticed, for instance, another neighbor whom I've never met, but one for whom I've gained a measure of sympathy. I have a couple of houseguests for a week, summer, and we've taken to watching him as we drink gin and tonics on my back deck, the side of the house facing away from Jerry, from the day care, from the dead man's house with the beautiful brick driveway. Over the week my guests have, like me, grown more interested in this particular neighbor. I ascribe it to their being on vacation and having time for such peeping; they ascribe it to the gin I'm serving them.

This neighbor Judkins, which is the name I've decided to give him, Judkins reminds me of the balding little man who is trapped in the basement in *Night of the Living Dead*, when the ghouls are gathering outside the boarded-up windows and doors of that Pennsylvania farmhouse. Judkins is nervous, too short. I am not a tall person and harbor no prejudice, but it seems that Judkins himself would prefer to be taller. He's bald on top, a ring of hair around his crown. He often clenches his fists, and talks with a slight lisp. His wife is taller and much bigger than he is. To be less politic: she is hugely fat, a mountain. They've been undertaking some kind of construction project on their back deck, and we often see her, not him, with power tools on a fold up workbench in the yard. Again, I have no skill with tools and so cannot be faulting Judkins for what seems his lack of ability. As I said, I'm sympathetic.

Our interest is that after a week of gin and tonics at cocktail hour, we can't figure out what in the world they might be building there. There seems to be a good deal of sawing of wood and driving of nails. There's a pile of scrap growing in the corner of the yard nearest to my elevated three-season porch. But not many signs of progress. And then after an hour or so the work will cease for a day, unfinished portions of the construction hid under the deck to keep them out of the rain.

Of course the family is loud, and now they've gotten a puppy which is staked to the ground in the back yard in front of a doghouse into which it's never ventured. Often it's tangling itself around its own leash or the posts holding up the deck. The dog whines, but never night or early morning, and it's small enough that it's not a problem yet.

I have to imagine that by next summer the dog will be gone. The family cannot seem to care for it. Why do I think that?

Maybe because the four children in the family seem to plague Judkins. Each of the three boys seems to pick mercilessly on the brother immediately younger than he, and the girl is the target of all but the littlest boy, who is the target of all. The most routine play ends time and again with one or more of the children crying, and no mercy shown by the others. The children have oversized orange plastic bats which they bang against each other in a play sword fight, making a loud and hollow popping sound. Yes, it's loud, but the family dynamic is too fascinating for me to be disturbed. The kids pound their plastic bats against the ground, against the posts holding up the deck, against everyone and everything except, thankfully, the dog. The kids frenetically run from one occupation of play to another, all four always shouting at once.

The large mother appears from time to time to lay down the law, and the kids stop and listen when she does. But always on the scene is the father, Judkins, who seems to have no authority over them. He's standing on the deck, almost never in the yard where the kids fight and play. Or audible from inside the patio door that leads into the kitchen. Or sitting on the floor of the deck, legs crossed at the ankles. There are two constants to his beleaguered presence: a cell phone, on which he talks quickly and loudly and from which one or more of the children, every moment or so, attempts to distract him. And a nervous cigarette, one of which he is forever smoking, held in thumb and first finger like a punk in a movie rather than more naturally between the first and second finger. It's strange that I can never hear what the man is saying on the phone, yet his voice seems always audible and his meaning clear. It's the voice of worry and agitation. A petulant, too-earnest tone. A mid-range but modulating pitch. Overenunciated, quietly desperate. In my view of the scene, it's never a nice day for Judkins. The children bother him for attention, but when he gives them orders in reply, they go about their ways as if he's not there.

And then sometimes later in the evening, Judkins' voice is the only one heard, no phone now. His volume is constant with rage, the pitch flattened to one note. An unformed, higher voice of one of the children will attempt to speak in defense, but it's cut short by the father's will, the one voice that carries through the neighborhood. A voice of anger.

One image seems to represent the whole family for me: the deck is empty, it's earlier in the evening's arc. The yard vacant, all are inside the house, all are talking at once, all yelling at once, and the father, amazingly, is still audible to me as he speaks on the cell phone. He's smoking inside the house, which I know the mother doesn't like, and I know this because at one point, needing both hands for something, the father Judkins slides open the patio screen, and closes it again so it holds the burning cigarette, pointing out towards the yard, a thin column of blue smoke rising from it. The cigarette is stuck there without a mouth to belong to for a moment. And seeing the smoke and hearing the talk, I know there is someone in the neighborhood worse off than me. Though not as bad off as Jack Kingsley.

My houseguests have left and now I watch alone. It's a warm day, and again the children play, each in a bathing suit, a middle boy holding a garden hose. I'm like Jimmy Stewart in *Rear Window*, not doing any real harm entertaining myself, but able to form my own conclusions. This time, the three oldest children have painted themselves with mud. All four are screaming and screeching as usual, shouting at once and at no one. There seems to be no reason or pattern to their play, or even to the angles they frantically run within the picket-fenced yard. They're like mice in a wall-less maze.

The second boy is holding the hose now and the eldest boy (probably younger than the girl, her body beginning to take its adult shape), this boy darts forward and pushes the middle brother sharply to the ground, grabs the hose, and turns it on the face of the youngest brother, who is maybe six years old.

The fat plastic orange bats the kids use to wop each other in the head and body (the littlest one always loses this battle too) lie still on the grass.

After the incident with the hose, the screaming of the two younger boys has turned to a loud wail of tears, one boy a victim of theft the other of violence. The screaming of the eldest boy and the girl has stopped for an instant as they listen to their siblings with fascination, or maybe satisfaction.

Often during such play, I have heard the sinus voice of the father carry out to the children from inside the house. But today it does not do so. The leafless April branches blow in the hot day wind.

※

Earlier today Jerry hailed Linda while she was out on the street to pick up our mail. Had she heard the neighborhood news? No news, Linda said. Despite my spying and conjecture, we pride ourselves on being the last to know what our neighbors are up to.

Had we noticed all the cars at James' house, next door to Jerry? I told Linda I had: cars coming and going at different hours, as if the family had a sideline business in cocaine. Well, it seems that weeks ago, Heather moved out once and for all, taking her new baby with her. James and the two daughters were left to abide at home. Improbable. Unexpected when you don't know, in the lives of others, what is really going on. You don't know the inner lives, who is the good guy and who the bad, and what strains of character run where and how deep. You can't judge finally, but only observe and withhold all but the judgment you can't resist making.

It came out somehow, Jerry reports, that James was not the father of the new baby his wife was carrying. The father was his best friend, around the house to help out while James served his country in the war away.

Now James' brother has moved into the house, to help with expenses

I suppose, the brother's girlfriend living there too, living in the basement, Jerry said. (I'm wondering if they all drive large SUVs, which would explain the car lot in the driveway.) The two brothers sometimes argue loudly, one night out on the back deck coming to blows until the police arrived.

And oh yeah, Jerry adds, James has a new girlfriend, too.

Now that he's pointed it out, I see all the signs, the new couple necking in the driveway, the way new lovers do, as he's off in the morning, coffee and business suit.

Jerry doesn't tell Linda how the neighborhood must look to him now. Or how the world looks. Nor do I tell him how the world looks to me, how much we can never know for sure, what moments unrevealed. "Baby Factory" was not that after all. Wrong stereotype. Her desires resided elsewhere, and now so does she.

✳

It's Halloween, and Linda and I are home that evening for the first time since we moved to New Brookside. So I decide to leave the porch and driveway lights on to invite kids to come to our door—though I doubt there will be many, here in the suburbs. Linda bought several bags of candy for the night on the condition that I would be the one to get up to answer the doorbell and dole it out. I scolded her for not buying candy that I like (which is to say candy with chocolate in it), sure that we would have most of it left at the end of the evening and I'd get to finish it.

The first group of kids comes to the door, some dressed as traditional ghosts and witches, most dolled up to look like pop culture figures I don't recognize, superheroes and animated princesses. Then the second batch comes and the third, and then more. It's dark now outside the perimeter of light coming from our homestead, dark between the lights from all the homesteads on the block that have invited kids to their door. Jerry Clark's light is on, as is James's. There's even a light on in front of the house where Jack Kingsley used to live. I haven't seen a for sale sign there, and I think maybe a relative has moved in, though I haven't gone over there to say hello.

By mid-evening Hansen Street is dotted with packs of kids, the lines of their movement ebbing and flowing with laughter. The larger groups of older kids come to the door unaccompanied; little kids and those just past being little, even little Black and Asian kids I'm happy to see, are all in costumes they're in danger of tripping over. The little ones are shadowed by a parent or often, I think, Grandpa or Grandma. Other than this adult presence, the scene is not much different from what I remember in my day. I'm pleased.

Our candy is almost gone when the bell rings for one of the last times. I'm a little tired of the routine by now, out of ways to express my surprise at costumes. I'm looking forward to a beer and ten o'clock news. At the door this time is a group of three girls, older than most of the kids who have come. The prettiest girl is dressed as a ballerina and smiles a perfect smile, not at me, but at the level of my hand reaching out to drop candy in her bag. She's really smiling for her two friends and for herself, probably their last time to go trick or treating, and probably they know this.

I'm thinking maybe I've seen the ballerina before, when I hear a voice from a largish adult in the shadow beyond my light.

"I'm Anne Judkins," the woman's voice says. "We live behind you, and haven't introduced ourselves yet. You know, the ones with the noisy kids back there!"

"That's right, we haven't met," I say, straightening my social mask. "And yeah, I've noticed those kids are very active. But I notice you know how to make them behave! I kind of like watching them."

It was all true. But I would see the oldest one a little less now, the pretty girl, Anne Judkins tells me. She will be busy babysitting the two little girls at James' house, right across the street.

"So you like living here then," Anne Judkins concludes. She sounds genuinely glad. The three trick-or-treaters have started to move on to the next house. Maybe they got a late start on their rounds.

"We've lived here more than three years already," I say.

The woman has stepped into the light, a solid brown coat and hair lying flat and thin. Just then a cell phone rings in her pocket.

"The time sure goes by, doesn't it?"

"You can't know how true that is," I say. It's good small talk, and in one moment, after they leave, I'll be glad that things are not always what they appear to be, and sometimes not worse than they appear. I'm glad that we can never know much for sure, and that I believe that.

"Phone!" the little girl shouts. She runs up from out of the shadow.

"It's probably just Dad."

ESSENTIALLY

"'Things were of course the sum of the world…. She could imagine people not having, but she couldn't imagine their not wanting and not missing."
—HENRY JAMES, *The Spoils of Poynton*

YESTERDAY WAS THE ANNUAL "CLEAN-UP DAY" IN NEW BROOKSIDE, our solidly middle-class burb. It's the day the city allows people to put out for collection at no extra charge things that would be too big for their trash cans. Each year, I find it a good day to extend my dog Zachy's walk to inspect what my neighbors have brought forth from their basements and garages. This one time a year, truth is lining the curbs.

Other years, I confess that I've driven around and stopped to fill the back of my car with stuff too good for the landfill, and brought it to the local thrift store for resale for some good cause. It's not so much that I'm environmentally woke, as that I'm my mother's son, and she never threw anything away. Neither did her father before her. They each lived through the Depression, and also shared something Northern and Germanic about economy making good sense. My grandfather had a place for everything, down to the smallest tack, nail, fruit jar—and could find it in his house even after he was mostly blind.

As I write, we're in what I presume to be Year One of the COVID Plague. With people locked down and little better to do, the ore of the discarded is especially rich this year. But with the virus at hand, too literally, I'm not about to go around touching everything for donation to the thrift store. "No thank you, we're just looking," I say to the dog.

And what do Zachy and I see on our walk? So many mattresses (illegal to resell)—as if the neighbors expect the homeless to spend a restful night in their yard. At least two perfectly good filing cabinets, made redundant in the digital age. Two sets of golf clubs, his and hers. Why do I suppose the shafts are bent with age, balls hooking into the rough or slicing into divorce? The inventory of appliances and gizmos that don't work, or so one assumes at first: box fans, refrigerator/freezers, window ACs, floor lamps, stationary treadmills, long-stilled clocks,

Lying closed on one guy's lawn: a door. Leading where?

Comic relief, standing six feet away from the rest of the items: a toilet. No modesty here.

So many toys that Johnnie and Susie have outgrown: jungle gyms, wading pools, bikes with colored streamers left hanging from the handlebars. Also pet carriers, portable coolers. I can't help but assess the condition of the things as we pass. Here's a dart board, pocked like the battlefield of an old war. Why did they keep it this long?

Much of the rest, though, seems serviceable. Or better. I couldn't know unless I plugged it in, tried it out. I want to.

Lumber, lots of lumber. And chairs, so many chairs: lounge, lawn, desk, dining room. Most have four legs and a seat intact. A visitor from another planet would assume everyone now prefers to stand.

Zachy stops at one neighbor's driveway to lift a leg on a pile of flotsam. I understand his thinking, but I pull him away. For it's about this point in the morning every year that I begin to see the less fortunate start their combing of our streets, with their old 4x4s and rusted SUVs, looking for what can furnish their lives, looking for what is, at least, better than what they have. They are our scavenger angels; I think of the trees and fields saved from excavation and fill. What might be thrift for me and tidying up for my neighbors is need for them. Some of their vehicles are filled to overflow and leave to come back for a second trip through the foreign neighborhoods.

But the scavengers too are fewer this year. As with everything else in our lives, this year is a little different. The "inessential" stores are closed. (You know the rest, alive now as you are.) Over this great neighborhood unfolding,

Marie Kondo rules; there is space freed at last in the homes of those refusing to fall from the middle class with everyone else. But why is it that the Depression my mother and grandfather lived through led them to look for the value, or at least the utility in things? While in my own times, an interruption in good fortune has led people to throw out much more than usual? An article in this morning's paper about "Spruce Up Days" in other towns says the same thing is happening everywhere. Is the purging simply because we have more time on our hands? Perhaps.

The dog has me stop at a collection of unmatched furniture. As my mother's son, and someone whose home is still furnished mostly with pieces I got when my mother died, I take a look. It seems that people put things on the curb mostly not because they no longer work, or not even because they no longer "spark joy." It's because the things have been replaced by new things, or will be once this interval of contagion has passed. Replace, not Reuse. Upgrade.

Aware of the passing of years, and not to think of myself as a hoarder (I'm not), I too wish to downsize. Each Clean Up Day I scan the basement shelves and shuffle through the garage. Today I found a few short, rotting boards from last season's raised garden beds, also a burned-out fluorescent bulb, and I put them out under the tree by the curb. Later that morning, I saw a trash guy pick up the boards. He had to leave the bulbs. I know, hazardous waste.

I'm not telling myself on this walk much that we all didn't know before. Even the dog now is less interested in an unopened bag of roofing shingles than he is in the trail of a long departed red squirrel. This year, there is plenty of misery and suffering in the air, with worse to come, no doubt. (I tell this to the dog, since he's the only one I know who hasn't heard it.) With the closings, the markets, the economies are going in the tank, reliant as they are on people buying things to replace what's lying at our feet.

Reliant, I think I see now, on people buying things they don't need. Why do they do it? I suppose because they can, we all can. The neighbors will buy, or have already bought, new chairs to replace those that will be buried in what once was a place to grow corn or pasture Holsteins. No one will be left standing. Not now, not when the music stops.

But little has been proven Essential. When we can buy only that which is essential, everyone loses their jobs. Could we not, then, all find more important work? Except that's not the way of the world.

As I said, we knew it all before the outbreak, didn't we? About our dependence on the life cycle and death rattle of stuff acquired to take our minds off... well, whatever it is. We've learned that "Everything's a dollar," but also that a dollar is everything—for what it will buy.

Like death, our own discarding, better not to speak of the end. For I think now, maybe I always thought, that all waste is hazardous, and our livelihoods, if not our lives, seem to depend on collecting and disposing. There are so many of us now, and so much of it.

WeChat ══════════════════════════

FORMER STUDENT OF MINE FROM THIRTY-FIVE YEARS AGO IN CHINA is visiting us in Minnesota, with her husband, and they are in the back seat of my car. We're driving through Iowa, on our way to Iowa City to see another former Chinese student who has worked now for years at the International Center at the University. Back in '85, Lu was one of the first in his class to join the Communist Party. He was, we might have said in America, a real boy scout—always thinking of others; helpful to me, the foreigner; and quick to repeat the slogans of the day: "Serve the people" and "Do you love the Party, comrade?" I wonder if in looking back, comfortable as he is now in "dog eat dog" America, as the Party called it, he finds it all at least a little embarrassing.

In those days, Peng Liying, who is the now-middle-aged woman in the backseat, once said about Lu, with an exaggerated inflection, "He is what we call a Good Communist!" and then the other young woman students present let out a quiet laugh, hidden behind their palms. The gesture may have had something to do with feminine propriety in the culture. Or maybe they weren't sure if it was permitted for a reference to Party loyalty to be considered funny.

Now Lu is an American citizen, lives in a lovely house, owns a couple of new duplexes which he rents out to visiting Chinese scholars that he meets through work. Americans might call him a self-made man. Peng Liying and her husband have invested in vacation property near the beach in Penang, Malaysia, and are about to build a new house in the suburbs in China. They're interested in the U.S. housing market as well, since their daughter is studying in New York and hopes to immigrate. Linda has taken them inside a couple of open houses in Minneapolis during their stay, so they could learn more about real estate here. I waited in the car, joking that I liked the house we lived in now just fine.

I knew Lu and Peng Liying when they and their classmates would wear their Mao jackets the one day a week that their one set of regular clothes was hanging out to dry in the coal-dark air of our provincial city. They were impoverished students then, but not terribly much poorer than anyone else in town. The gray and brown tones of the city were so prevalent that wandering around without a reading knowledge of Chinese, I couldn't tell restaurants from auto repair shops. All were seemingly lit by a single bare bulb. Then about ten years ago, Linda and I returned to Baoding to find, as the cliché about China goes, everything changed. I could still identify my old apartment building, but the University had built an entirely new campus on the edge of town. Word was they put up the whole thing in about a year. Most notably, whereas in my day travel in Baoding was by rusted bus or donkey cart, the city now boasted a Mercedes Benz dealership.

Here, these decades after our time together, it's a mild June day—a nice time of year to visit the American Midwest. I might say that the landscape is rolling by as we drive—except this is Iowa. Can I say the landscape is *flattening* by as we drive? There is corn/crossroads/corn, not much to see, so Peng Liying is holding her phone in front of my face while I drive (Straight roads and little traffic, so not as dangerous as it sounds. Did I mention we're in Iowa?)

On the phone, another former student, now the Director of Foreign Affairs at a top-five Chinese university, wants to say hello on WeChat. Is this really happening? I think. A link to my past via the devices of what was once the future? I'm driving and looking at the magic phone.

How are you Terrill have you eaten you are still our teacher. Not long after the obligatory pleasantries, Chen the Director gets a glimmer in her eye and reaches to her office bookshelf. The book she takes down is my own, *Saturday Night in Baoding: A China Memoir.* When I wrote and published it, it seemed impossible that she or any of my other students in China would ever see it, and that surely influenced what I wrote. But then, who in 1985 would have predicted small telephones that carried snow-free images and clear sounds from across the planet?

Chen looks at her phone camera and reads my own words for me as the cornfields fly by.

Soon I began to find out from the better gossips among the students that even the girls I thought didn't have boyfriends, have.

The I, of course, the narrator, is me—lonely young man on that other side of the world. Only a few years their senior, I was in love with all of my young women students, and it was the "all" which made it harmless, innocent (as strange as that may sound now, in another culture and time). How stripped bare to have your words read back to you. It's a little embarrassing. I was "teacher," and to the Chinese that means I will always be.

I go on driving. What choice do I have? I know Chen's read the whole book, most of the students have. They've read the part where, upon my arrival, my dean says to me, "The girls ... try to stay away from them. They get crushes very easily." They've read the parts after that, many parts, where I wonder, if I were to break my word to the dean, which of these young women would I ask to come home with me?

I was a good and fair-minded reporter. But not until the last chapter did I learn I was coming already too late to the dance. Chen reads on:

Xie Rong, an affair with a teacher in the Philosophy Department for two or three years now. Another senior girl choosing between two different ones, one here and one away. Another having a secret boyfriend no one was supposed to know about yet, but everyone did. Another. Another.

Chen closes the book and begins to laugh—openly now, no need to hide anything. Xie Rong was Chen—I changed names, but I wasn't fooling anyone as to who was who. That older man from another department is now her husband of these many years. I think she's teasing me, that what I sounded so forlorn about then, now seems quite humorous. But what exactly *is* she laughing at? Laughing that she has now spent half a lifetime with the man I described? Laughing at the foreigner's misapprehension of things, always at the arm's length of culture? Laughing at his confession, his heart on a sleeve for any reader to see? I am part hopeless romantic, part clueless outsider.

Had I not been that character in the play, I might have laughed too, the way the Chinese do to ease an uncomfortable moment, when you're not sure if something is funny yet. Instead, I smile and keep on driving.

Chen completes her greeting to "our dear teacher" (as I said, that adoration for the elder hasn't changed.) Peng Liying draws her phone back from my point of view. The two of them chat a bit more in Mandarin, then, I imagine, a talk-to-you-later leave taking.

"This technology. What a world!" I exclaim loudly, to be heard in the back seat, noting that letters from home had sometimes taken weeks to get to me in Baoding. I'm trying to change the subject, but it doesn't quite work because on this new subject, there's little more to say. We all know about change, how it is inescapable. Marx and the Chinese Communist Party had been right about that. So had F. Scott Fitzgerald, the Buddha, Jim Croce, Robert Burns, Shakespeare and a host of others. How little I had known then—of what was to come, but also of what *was*. Things happen around us, out of our ken. Or as Lu had told me on an earlier visit I made to Iowa City, "Your book—it was interesting to hear... *the way you saw things.*" He was being polite, but that was a more honest appraisal than I got from some reviewers.

My wife, in the front passenger seat, is from Hong Kong. (Once home from Baoding, I didn't set out to marry a Chinese, but things happen the way they will.) For thirty years now, people who get to know us have been disappointed that the two of us met in a small town in southern Minnesota, not in faraway China.

Linda is a native Cantonese speaker but self-taught in Mandarin and quite good at it. So after the magic phone call to China ends, the conversation between the three of them, Linda, Peng Liying, and her husband, goes on, lively and fun. This is a road trip after all, if a monotonous one. I know barely enough Chinese to pick out common expressions and form words from their talk. "That's interesting." "Far from here." "Not far from here." "*Wo de*"—mine. "*Ni de*"—yours. At times, I can I get a vague idea of what they're talking about. I could ask Linda later, and she might remember.

"You know, if you had a steady job back in the States, I think you would have found that many of the girl students would have wanted to go home with you." My dean waited until the end of my year in China to make this confession to me. As it turns out, though, those girls wouldn't have needed to make the trip, wealthier than us as many of them are now. And no doubt almost as comfortable, even living as they do in a crowded place so unlike the open spaces we drive past.

It seems we have all found a relative comfort in our later years. My book on China won a big prize and because of that I got a good teaching job at home; no more running around the world to find work. And my students learned English at a time in China when English was most in demand, and many of them made their fortunes. And yes, most joined the Communist Party, the path to advancement. We helped each other, and life traverses the unpredictable paths of least resistance, with a nod toward the vagaries of chance. It's another dynamic we can't recognize in real time, like secret love affairs. Maybe we don't have a lot to be embarrassed about.

We've got an hour's drive more to Iowa City. Outside the window, the cornfields, unchanged and unchanging, make us feel that for hours we haven't gotten anywhere at all.

Going to the Dogs

MY DOG COSMO IS DEATHLY AFRAID OF STORM SEWERS. THE KIND that hold a grate over a deep, dark hole he finds especially terrifying. When he spies one, at around twenty feet away, he'll crouch down belly to the road—"pancake" is how the trainer at the Humane Society described it—and begin to back away on his leash. No treat will get him to change directions and continue our walk. I pull myself closer and have to lift him up and carry him past the object of his terror.

Cosmo is all of seventeen pounds, or about one fifth the size of an average German Shepherd. He's one of those terrier types whose hair feathers down over his eyes, as if he can't quite help it. His skinny legs are long out of proportion to his body, like some miniature white greyhound. When we walk, the top of his head is barely level with my knee. With us now six weeks, a rescue from a local agency, Cosmo has been calm when safe in the house. He loves a good nap, likes to run off with a sock or a pair of undies and dare us to catch him. He'll fetch a tennis ball I throw from room to room—over and over…and over and over. I still haven't found the point at which he tires of it.

But Cosmo still has accidents, even if he usually tries to hide the evidence of them by doing his business in a corner of the basement. He will roll on his back for a belly rub—maybe because he likes the attention, but maybe as a gesture of submission. There is still some distance about him I can't quite describe. He is *with* us but not exactly *of* us. The remedy might be just a little more time to get acquainted

On the leash, though, Dr. Cosmo becomes Mr. Hyde, and that's a problem that's not going away by itself. As Cosmo and I leave the house this morning, the neighbor's delivery man is the object of suspicion. Cosmo emits a low growl and muffled bark. Meanwhile, unseen by either of us, a golden retriever and his owner come marching toward us from the other direction. This sends Cosmo into his red zone. He leaps and barks, rears to his hind legs like a wild horse, pulling against his supposedly no-pull harness. There's little I can do except drag him back into the house for a time out. I'm not about to let him disturb the neighborhood the way other neighbor dogs once did.

His spasms and gyrations on walks can seem comical to some. "Hey, Cujo!" one passing young man laughed at us yesterday. But others who pass give me a shaming look. *Why don't you train your dog?* Why indeed?

Cosmo is about one year old. We think. All we know for sure is that he was found wandering in the woods in Missouri, lost with another dog even younger and smaller, a shihzu mix. "What did you do those nights in the woods by yourself," my wife Linda asks our little troublemaker, his paws up on her waist, looking for attention. "Were you scared?"

I wonder even more what his life was like those months before he was abandoned, living with the kind of people who would eventually drop two cute little dogs at the side of the road and drive away. When first with us, Cosmo would stop at the threshold to the house—had he not been allowed indoors? Did the owners abandon him because winter was at hand and he wouldn't survive outside in the cold? And then there's that fear of storm sewers which I notice extends to any zebra-like pattern: the slats in an iron banister, the shadow of a picket fence in new snow. Was Cosmo kept in a kennel that had become a prison to him, that held some terror that still resides in memory?

※

People shouldn't write about their pets. I know that. Nor should they tell funny stories about their pets at already stultifying dinner parties. The only thing worse in those settings is people telling funny stories about their grandchildren, where if they talk about one kid, it's only fair to give equal time to the other five or six. This takes guests past dessert into that sleepy time that a full stomach and too much cabernet can engender. Both the dog tales and the grandkid stories are stocked with cutsie detail; both omit inconvenient truths about pooping, crying, and misbehavior. But to me the dog stories always ring more true, which may say more about me than it does about dogs. And even if the dog stories don't ring true, people usually have only one dog.

The true stories are ones like mine, of course. Like this one: Cosmo, strangely, has a talent for retrieving which would be more native to a golden or a lab than to a terrier/poodle mix (plus whatever else he is—bichon, Maltese, juvenile delinquent?) I know we didn't teach him to fetch. Neither did the cretin who abandoned him in the Ozarks of southern Missouri. But no matter where genetically he picked up this doggy aptitude, he also picked up a less common canine penchant for divergent thinking. He hides his toy bones in our shoes and then can't find them again. He drinks water from a watering can while his dish is full in the next room. He won't sit on my lap, but he will sit tentatively on my feet.

And then there's this, the prime example: when Cosmo had his first encounter with a lake, we could see his delight at learning that a paw lowered to the water's surface would continue through what he thought was a barrier to this fascinating underworld. We'd throw a stick and Cosmo, predictably, would gallop into the lake to bring it back. If the stick happened to float out to deeper water, he simply found another stick closer in and proudly returned that one for deposit. But then not waiting for our next throw, Cosmo started to pick up sticks *from the shore* and carry them out *to* the water, dropping them, and then turning to us waiting for praise.

I couldn't deny the logic of it. If he's that smart (isn't everyone's dog smarter than everyone else's?), maybe he's trainable. Except for what I knew about dog training, which was nothing.

Our previous dog Zachy, the one who could recognize the sound of my saxophone even on a recording, was another fluffball about the size of his successor. But Zachy came to us fully trained, from a family member who couldn't keep him. Zachy was also the only dog Linda and I had ever had. In fact, I used to dislike dogs, found their barking a sign of arrogance in the neighbors who owned them. I didn't yet understand how an animal with a robotic devotion to a master could be of much interest. Until the easygoing Zachy changed my thinking.

After picking up Cosmo from his foster, I simply assumed the sequel would follow smoothly from the first film in the series. Cosmo would be "Zachy II." No need to reacquaint with characters and follow a new plot. Then on our first walk around the neighborhood, Cosmo went doggy-postal at the mere sight of another dog or even of another person walking a block away. Given the same, Zachy would not as much as lift his nose from the ground. We were no longer reading from the same old script.

"What was I going to do?" I worried to friends. The main reasons I wanted to have a dog were to take long walks and to have my dog curl up on my lap in the evening. Cosmo would do neither. Could we keep this dog?

I called the rescue agency to ask advice. I researched online. Finally I called the training school at the Animal Humane Society, where I had volunteered for several years as a dog walker. I had learned something about dogs there, but hadn't walked many shelter dogs that had Cosmo's level of anxiety on a leash. I found that the shelter had a class called "Reactive Rovers" that seemed perfect for our little head case. What I wondered was, how could a reactive dog like Cosmo be in a class with other reactive dogs without, well, reacting? Cosmo, it turned out, was such a hard case that he had to have individual counseling sessions before even being admitted to the class with other reactive dogs…

…ah, but at this point in my tale, I'll stop to remind myself of the danger of stories about pets or grandchildren. Even a captive audience (those dinner parties, or engaged readers) needs to be freed from behind the invisible fence of their attention. I promise to get to the point. Quickly. And unlike those dinner party narratives, I promise to have a point….

…Flash forward: Despite his need for remedial instruction, Cosmo got his diploma from Reactive Rovers in the same graduating class as the other nervous and crazy dogs enrolled. It's now affixed to our refrigerator (right next to the picture of our granddaughter's first birthday party). It was too much to expect his behavior on the leash would change after only a few short sessions. It didn't. And no diplomas were offered to the dog *owners* attending. The main thing Cosmo and I learned in the class was that I was the one who needed to be trained.

Lack of patience. Lack of discipline. Weariness and wariness with consistency. Repetition always suggested to me the military, which I had worked hard to avoid in the Vietnam War days of the draft in my youth. I didn't even like marching band in high school. I was more a guy who could carry a stick from the shore into the lake and look up expecting praise. So it was a big step for me to switch my volunteer role at the Humane Society from Dog Walker to Training Assistant in the very training school that had shown Cosmo wasn't totally hopeless.

I needed to be trained to train my dog. For weeks I watched beagles go-to-mat on cue. Pit bulls perform on-duty walks with perfect turns. Shibus and Pomeranians run to find their owners hiding behind baffles at the far end of the training school gym. I would take the class exercises home and find that, without much of the daily practice I found so tedious, Cosmo performed most of them right away. I'd give the hand signal for Sit or Down or Go To Bed, and he'd comply and look at me like, "Duh??" and wait for his treat. I figured I wouldn't have to invest a lot of time on these commands he picked up so quickly.

I was wrong, though. On walks, Cosmo would still go ballistic at the sight or scent of any sentient being who came within a hundred feet of our path. It seems my signature impatience had gotten the best of both of us.

"What your dog needs," the training school teacher told me after class one day, "is Relaxation Protocol." He directed me online to a fifteen-day regimen meant to build trust between the dog and his human. Each day's work required about twenty-five tasks the dog was to perform. When each step was completed, the human was to praise the dog and, of course, add a treat. If the dog did something he wasn't supposed to, most commonly getting up and walking away, you had to start over on that day's list the next day. "My dog Zero took a few weeks to get through the whole course," the trainer told me; I imagined that for Cosmo, the 15-day course could take forever. Forever was not on my dance card. But by now I loved the little guy and had to give it a go.

Day One's tasks began simply enough:

Sit for 5 seconds

Sit for 10 seconds

Sit while you take 1 step back and return

Sit while you take 2 steps back and return

Sit for 10 seconds

Sit while you take 1 step to the right and return

Sit while you take 1 step to the left and return

"Duh," Cosmo said again. "Feed me." It was easy, even though my part of the game made me feel like I was doing the Hokey Pokey. And the regimen was more challenging than it might appear, given the 25 odd steps in each day's routine. I wondered if given the reverse and Cosmo were training me, would I be able to move on to Day Two any sooner than he had? Depends on the treats I was offered, I suppose. An all-expense paid week in the Bahamas? Hey, I'm there. Half of a Milk-bone? No way.

But we persevered. Which is to say I persevered, and Cosmo never tired of the high-end, top shelf bacon flavored training bits, each broken into six parts so he wouldn't put on weight by consuming 25 of them a day for what I thought might be months on end.

By the time we got to Day 15, the last day, the price of poker had gone up.

Sit for 15 seconds while you clap your hands and hum

Sit while you disappear from view, knock or ring the doorbell, say "hello," talk for 10 seconds, and return

Sit for 20 seconds while you hum

Sit while you disappear from view, say "hello," invite an imaginary person in, wait 5 seconds, and return

Sit while you leave the room and knock or ring the doorbell for 5 seconds

Sit while you leave the room and talk for 3 seconds to people who are not there

I wasn't sure about the part that had me talk to imaginary people (and do so presumably while sober). I thought for reasons of mental health this was a skill I shouldn't learn too well. For his part, Cosmo could never get past the doorbell stuff (What good dog could?), so each of us took a mulligan on this last day. I declared victory on Day 14, happy the therapy stopped at that point. What might a Day 16 have brought? Day 20?

> Have your dog levitate while you recite the Gettysburg Address
>   backwards from the garage
>
> Sit while you clap three times then vaporize, resubstantiating
>   as a fire hydrant

No way. Even before Day 14, Cosmo and I were in deep water, and we both knew it. Every so often when I left the room to answer the door to no one there, he'd sneak away from his bed and peer at me from around a corner in the next room. I pretended I didn't see it. As it was, the two weeks of exercises had taken us about a month and half. But after all the hard work, it was gratifying that now when I walked Cosmo on the leash through the neighborhood, he was...

...not as bad as he used to be.

If we encountered another living creature on our route, he'd whine and shiver, sometimes stifle a bark or two, but then fix his eyes on mine, waiting for his treat. Fully trained, I quickly slipped him a cookie. And then turned around and headed in the other direction.

No, I will never be able to take Cosmo to the county fair or to mingle with the crowds outside a Twins game. But the truth is we don't like county fairs, neither of us. Baseball is better on TV. And some people deserve to be barked at. As trained as he's going to get, Cosmo still does mostly what he wants. But he less often does what I don't want. Turns out we are perfect for each other. Cosmo doesn't have any more discipline than I do.

"Sorry, kid," I tell him as he makes a wide circle around another neighborhood storm sewer. Then we head for home.

*

We're living in an era of *canine philia*. Dog ownership is steadily rising; you can google the statistics as easily as I can: 75 million dogs in U.S. households. The dozens of books in the local library with titles like *The Emotional Lives of Animals* and *A Dog's World* are always checked out. Hollywood movies posit reincarnation—that if you own dogs through your lifetime, the dog you had as a kid will eventually find you generations hence. And writers indulge themselves in stories like the one I've just let go on longer than I promised.

Is carrying this cultural attitude toward pets who, after all, are "only animals," hopelessly bourgeois? Of course it is. So are our SUVs, our oversized homes, our lawns (though mine is a bee yard!), our car-dependent suburbs. In summer we crank the AC; in winter we eat blueberries from Chile. Minnesotans fly south to beat the January cold, leaving a vapor trail of CO2.

It is precious, anthropomorphizing, maybe even pathetic to feel, as we do now, that our animals are "part of the family." Are we dog lovers in denial about something greater and deeper missing in our lives? Yes, but are there not more damning sins? Make the list for yourself. Look inside first.

During COVID, with people trapped in their homes, the pace of dog (and cat) adoptions at the Humane Society where I volunteered quickened noticeably. Empty kennels lined the walls. Volunteer shifts ended early since there wasn't enough to do. When Linda and I decided to look for a rescue ourselves to replace our recently departed Zachy, we had to put in an application for an animal sight unseen within minutes of it appearing on the adoption website. Hesitate, and Fido was spoken for. It was like trying to buy a house in San Francisco if, thankfully, less expensive. Working from home, bored at not going out, everybody suddenly wanted a dog.

When the pandemic subsides, to whatever degree it eventually will, when people return to the office and are able to travel and party and stay out late, will there be a rate-of-return to match the pace at which the dogs went out the shelter doors? From what I read and hear, it may be starting already. If you find that the new pants are too snug in the waist, you simply ship them back to Amazon, or visit the customer service desk, no questions asked.

No one can be too surprised at what may turn out to have been Rent-A-Pet. More compelling is the thought that a phenomenon the inverse of this one could never come about. If *dogs* were *our* keepers, they wouldn't give up on us and take us back like ill-fitting sweaters. No investment banker with sad eyes would be surrendered because he soiled the carpet or barked whenever guests came for dinner. No shoe clerk with matted hair would be abandoned to wander in the Ozarks with only a smaller and more innocent-looking tax accountant for company. No registered nurse would once again peer out from a kennel, waiting to find home.

Those of us who keep dogs know that, unlike many of the people of our acquaintance, the dogs would never leave us. It's not because the dogs would feel bad or guilty returning us to the pound. We might deserve it, for one thing, and they're not capable of feelings that extend far beyond habit and comfort and the needs of the day. It's just that they wouldn't do it, and we know we would.

When I worry about the collapse of the natural world and what that portends for our species, I sometimes don't particularly mind that humans may someday disappear from the planet—as cold hearted as that sounds. We've had our evolutionary run and we deserve the environmental bed we will lie in. It bothers me, though, that we'll be taking so many wonderful species down with us. It's happening now. The three billion birds gone missing from North America in my lifetime. Even all those insects that used to smudge the windshields on car trips in summer nights—gone, and we know now that the rest of life depends on them.

I wonder if the popularity of pets in a country in denial about this Sixth Mass Extinction, about climate change and the overpopulation and overconsumption that drives it, is due to some unconscious guilt. We can't save the last male white rhino in some faraway reserve, but we can take home and love that one shy collie/shepherd mix with the doleful eyes. Maybe the run on adoptable dogs during COVID was not only due to human boredom and selfishness, but also to some guilt about the animals we *couldn't* adopt. No polar bears sleeping at the foot of the bed. No pangolins curled up in comfort by the gas fireplace. What we know about any dog is that, given an unlucky station in life, he almost certainly didn't deserve it. His care seems like the least we can do.

I promised I'd have a point to my dog story, and I may have succeeded not wisely but too well; I know that "Apocalypse" is another topic not welcome at most dinner parties, and more than many readers would bargain for. On a cheerier note, I recently read a newspaper article in which biologists posited that if humans did disappear from the planet, dogs might manage to survive without us. Dogs are pack animals, the piece read, and "different breeds of different sizes and aptitudes might band together for cooperative hunting."

Dog owners interviewed were sure their pets would do just fine:

"People with spitz breeds (including Alaskan malamutes and Samoyeds) had no doubts about their dogs' ability to survive. The same was true of people with Jack Russell terriers, some herding breeds or mixed breeds. Even dogs with disabilities might have a chance. 'My paraplegic dachshund probably has the best odds,' one person said. 'She's sneaky and remarkably fast.'"

There they go again, these humans telling their stories about their dogs, so smart they could get by without us. I think that given their choice, though, the dogs would prefer to have us around. Someone to whom the ball can be returned. Someone who will grant praise even for the stick dropped in the lake. I wonder if we can ever measure up, be worthy of the care the dogs would give us. Are we trainable, and is there enough discipline in the lot of us to complete the many lessons of the protocol before we're sent on our way?

THE VANTAGE

THE OTHER DAY I WENT OUT TO RAKE SOME WOOD CHIPS FROM THE spot where a city crew had dug out a dying ash tree. It was barely April in Minnesota and the job didn't need doing yet. But the temperature had broken 40 degrees and getting out is something we do around here to mark that passage.

I'd hardly begun when a younger guy I'd never met, thirty-something and the one renter on the block, the guy with the truck so big that most people would need a step stool to get in—that guy came over with a rake. "Want some help?"

Nonplussed is a word no one uses any more, but I need it to describe my reaction. "Naah, I was just going to rake the wood chips," I stammered. "That's all, twenty minutes, leave the dead leaves for mulch. Underneath is all clover for the bees, anyway."

More information than he needed. He'd brought along his rake and started in. We bagged the chips in no time, and he turned to leave.

"Let me know if *you* ever need anything," I said, and he turned back and nodded.

"I mean,…anytime," I added. (Just what *did* that mean?)

That night over dinner, with little else to report, I told Linda that the guy with the noisy truck came over to help me rake, and I couldn't understand why.

Then understanding popped into my head.

He came because I'm an old guy. He saw the thin shock of graying blonde, the scraggly beard. He didn't see, under my heavy spring coat, the weight shifting toward the middle, as if trying to match some kind of bell curve. Maybe that much he could guess.

What he saw taking place in my yard was different from what I was seeing looking out from that vantage.

I then realized that my fifty-year-old family doctor shares my neighbor's vantage point and treats me the same way. After a recent appointment, he called me at home to see how I was doing. On a Sunday. I'm doing fine, why wouldn't I be?

From his point of view, there was reason to wonder.

*

I'm 66, or only 66, depending, again, on your particular vantage, so let's get that out of the way. Let's skip the creative-writing-class anecdotes that would be so easy to insert at this point in my narrative: how, two years older than my wife, I laughed the first time I was able to get a senior discount at the movies and she couldn't. How not many years before that she laughed when she got carded at a cocktail lounge and I didn't. The stranger who, when I said I'd turned sixty, partly asked but mostly said, "Yeah, but how old do you feel?" and I answered, "60."

A few months later, a work colleague hit the big six oh and his wife said I should stick my head in his door and say something. "60, eh?" I commiserated. "It's the only one that ever bothered me."

I had a point, and so did that stranger. The important changes with aging are the ones that happen inside—but they're only important if you own up to them. I suspect the guy who coined the phrase "you're only as old as you feel" was in the marketing department somewhere. That adage assumes that if you indeed do *feel* your age, there is something wrong with you. It assumes, probably correctly, that people who feel old don't buy as much stuff as people who still think they have endless years before them.

But back to the changes inside—mind, heart, soul, whatever you wish to believe in. I was in my early twenties when my father reached retirement age and left his job. The two of us were fishing up at our family cottage. I was into staying up half the night, which you're not supposed to do on a fishing trip, and he being the age he was, could not stay awake past 10:30 (I've now come to understand.) I was sitting in front of the fireplace, probably with a drink in my hand cuz why not, and in between the crackles of poplar, I could hear my dad whispering in bed. The cabin had thin knotty pine walls, and only a curtain closing off the room.

My god, he was praying. Except for a mumbled Lord's prayer in church, I'd never heard such a thing from him.

I was embarrassed. I still might be. But more embarrassing is that at the time, I thought I understood why when they got old, people who weren't otherwise, got more religious. It made sense: death was nearer, and suddenly eternal life didn't seem like such a bad gig.

Oh callow youth! I'm starting to realize, just before my sixty-seventh birthday next week (yeah, pal, but how old do you *feel*?!?), that this praying need not be a cover-your-bets late conversion. What older people might pray for when considering their time left on the planet, is not their own souls. It's the planet. It's everybody else's soul—or more accurately everyone else's awareness in the here and now, which may be the same thing.

This prayer need not be whispered words in a little shack in the woods, but could as soon be a diary entry, an unwritten letter, or an answer to a bad dream that brings you to consciousness too early one morning. It need not be addressed to a god; an old photograph, a screaming newspaper headline, or a bottle of Jack Daniels will work just as well.

Now it's my turn to pray for the people who will be around after I'm gone, that the things that I care about—everything from wilderness and fresh water to mud turtles and bullfrogs, to free expression, the middle class, and rich complexity in music and the arts—all will still be there for somebody else. Otherwise, how will those people know what they've missed? Just as in my father's eyes, I can't know what I missed.

Older, you also care about your legacy, but that's a different essay. Or maybe this caring about what's dear in the otherwise difficult world, that which might be disappearing with you, is the legacy.

✳

The real curse of age is not that you'll never check the items off your bucket list (the guy who came up with that formulation, another marketing pro, how much money did he make?) It's not that you can't remember what you had for breakfast. Not that if you don't exercise, it hurts, but if you do exercise, it hurts more. These are all the stereotypes, true but not very interesting.

The real curse is that, even if you believed always in the inscrutability of life, nearer its end you become more *sure* of some things. For instance, just reread these pages. Do they hold the words of a young Hamlet, riddled with doubt? Seems not.

These things you're more sure of—they feel like the weight of the world, and it's up to you to carry the load, and you're running out of time. These are things about which you're convinced no one younger is ever going to see for the truth:

—The best run of American movies since the thirties ended with that stupid *Star Wars*.
—Pop music died in about 1949.
—Good pitching is a lot more interesting than good hitting.

OK, I'm joking here, even if I am right. But before you write me off as merely comic, enter these further items in my personal certainty column. (Note that they're all questions; I'm still hoping to learn…)

—Why do so few seem to recognize that climate change, and the most recent pandemic for that matter, are simply nature telling us there are too many people on the planet? Why when I point out that connection in polite company do other people look at me like I'm some kind of Nazi doctor?
—Why do we judge the past by the values we hold today (e.g. *because those patriarchal Founding Fathers owned slaves, they have nothing to offer us.*)? Should we not instead fear that the future will judge *us* by the values people will hold *then*? Do we suppose they'll think us enlightened, as we drive around in our SUVs and reproduce ourselves until other species disappear because there's nowhere left for them to live?

—Why do people now associate their "identity" more with their fore-bearers than with their own actions and values in this life?

And then this item, the golden rule of the hasty (yet true) generalization:

—"It's the rich against the poor, it always has been and it always will be."

The line sounds like it was uttered by Karl Marx over a beer, doesn't it? You can almost hear his fist hitting the café table, in German no less. But the great thinker who uttered those words was not Karl and not me. It was George Carlin. So don't be too tough on comedians. Or old guys, since when Carlin said that, he was about as old as he was going to get.

Yes, I can deconstruct my own rhetoric here and save you the trouble: *these formulations bear inflections characteristic of what theoretical linguistics call "the crotchety mood": note the plethora of questions to which the inquisitor already thinks he knows the answer. Note the implied exclamation points, the indictment of the unidentified listener—why don't/why can't. Note the breathless catalogue not allowing time for response. All endemic to the sub species,* veteris gaseous, *known in the vernacular as "the old fart."*

But I stand by every word. For now. As I said, I'm still open to correction.

And I know I'm not the only senior afflicted with the disease of late-life certainty. Consider this scene, in which I'm arguing on email with my oldest friend, part of a group of us who've been friends for 55 years. (Note too that we still use email.) The other friends are privy to our exchange, but know better than to jump in when the two of us go at it. We're arguing about who was the more damaging president, Trump or Reagan. I'm arguing the latter (at the time of the exchange, Trump still had time to pull ahead.)

My friend lists his obvious reasoning for voting Trump the worst, and then in one of those one-sentence paragraphs that is so declamatory, so proud of itself (like the one sentence graphs I'm fond of using in this essay), my friend adds,

"I know I'm right."

"Well," I write, "I guess that ends the discussion."

*

Here's another way to look at it. To be specific, the viewpoint of a twenty-three-year-old. Me, forty-three years ago, needing extra money in grad school to support my scant salary as a teaching assistant. A friend sets me up with a gig he already has, teaching a creative writing class at a senior citizens' center. It's easy work, he says. And this being Tucson, Arizona, the people are mostly snowbirds, people who seem more interested in pleasant diversions than in giving a lot of thought to most things, God bless them.

I remember only two things about that class. One is that in the next room from mine, same hour, there was a woman teaching conversational Spanish who was so remarkably, untouchably beautiful that I would linger a bit outside the window of her classroom door. She always wore a colored knit cap (this was winter, and for Arizonans, the January mornings qualified as chilly.) She was as slender as winter light, dark hair and dark complexion. And she was always smiling—glowing, actually—as were most of her senior students. Why wouldn't they be?

The reason I remember her is likely that it reminds me how a young man sees the world.

The other thing I remember was one of my students. He was a retired truck driver who looked the part—stocky not like someone built that way but like someone who became that way. Bald with thin gray hair short cropped around the sides. A full round face, and not unpleasant disposition. He had a way of talking in class that would start in one place and end in one very different, and the rest of us with no map of how he got there. As if his big rig were toting a load of daydreams.

The truck driver's writing was in piles of single-spaced pages, this in the days of manual typewriters, remember. It was clearly not revised, maybe not even reread. No matter what kind of exercise I presented in class—write a poem that's only images, tell a story about a time you were proven wrong—the truck driver's submissions the following week were comprised entirely of his opinions. Not in a list, but in a winding progression that picked up a load in one place and brought it to market far, far away. He said he'd submitted the five- or ten-page pieces to the local paper's editorial page, and "they never printed a word of it."

But like my friend, he knew he was right. It was the one thing about each of his essays you could understand.

I suppose today those ramblings would be all about government and conspiracy and the truth behind the most recent outrage. Of what it was all about in 1975 I have no memory, and I probably couldn't tell at the time. Only that in his mind and on the page, the issues were all *connected*—the powerful rich, and water for desert cities, and the ungodly Tucson traffic, and the wisdom of further space travel. Or whatever it was.

Here's the thing. There's always *the thing*, isn't there, and most often not just one? The thing is that unlike the truck driver I can write clearly; I'm educated, too much, if perhaps not all that well; and I've never driven an eighteen-wheeler.

But I don't want to become that truck driver. I don't want to espouse only my opinions even if they could save the world, or save the planet, or at least save that lake I fished with my dad. I don't want to start in one place and end up in another and not know how I got there.

✳

Wisdom, of course, is learning that there's so much we don't know. Peace may be coming to terms with that very mystery. For as certain as we may grow about things that we hope–or yes, pray—that others will realize before shit hits the cosmic fan, we also realize with years that we don't know very much at all.

(Even though we know more than most people).

As tough as things might get personally, the best reason not to put your mouth to your tailpipe as you grow older is that it's going to be so interesting *to see what happens.* To see just *how* what you knew would happen, happens. Or maybe to be shown that you were wrong. But more importantly, to be shown why.

Some thinkers posit that the world stopped making sense around the beginning of the previous century, when things became "modern"— Einstein, T.S. Eliot, global war, and all that—and that we've been scratching our heads ever since. Mark that down in defense of confusion. That our confusion coincides *with the rise of international capital and the concurrent explosion in human numbers* leads me again down my road of certainty. Enough of that. The truck driver, I think now, was only trying to make sense of things, make those connections that explain the what and the why of it. And thereby maybe understand the world, even if still not understanding how his life turned out the way it did, why the things that seemed a sure bet when he was young and promising never happened. Or maybe it's my life, not his, I'm talking about—the unpublished books, the books unwritten, and even those that never needed to be.

The more unsure we are with age of what happened to us and why, the more we cling to the notions of what needs to be righted with the world. We know now we might be able to help, if only people understood, if only we could make the connections clear. Convincing.

But try as we might, those connections, and that satisfaction, will always elude us.

I know I'm right.

AUNTS: A REMEMBRANCE

T
HE HOUSE IS FULL OF AUNTS—*ANTS*, WE SAID IT, LIKE THE INSECT. The aunts leave red lipstick on the filters of their cigarettes, snubbed out in a free-standing ashtray. They bend low to hug the eight-year-old (*"Ricky, how you've grown."*) They smell of gin, Camay, and department stores. They cackle during a second cocktail, or retire en masse to the living room to talk about whatever the uncles don't.

They teach guitar or take dictation. They counsel wisely, make the rules. One aunt lives in a small guest house in the back—maybe it used to be a garage; one lives next door to a house that resembles an ice cube; another lives in one of those arrangements even stranger to a kid in a small midwestern city, circa the late nineteen fifties: *an apartment!* There is only one door from the outside, and then many doors leading to separate lives within. How do they get out to play? How do they not track wet snow down the hall?

My father had four sisters and one brother. My Aunt Gladys divorced Earl Gigler before the War. Aunt Vivian divorced Harry Pierquet during the War. (I'd heard once she had another quick husband after that, but older cousins said otherwise and are probably right.) Aunt Mildred divorced Mervin Brunette after the War, but then there was Tom, the likeable oaf who happened along years later in Mildred's life, in my era. He came to family parties for years, to us kids just another uncle, another present at Christmastime. "Why don't you *marry* him Mildred," the other aunts and even the uncles said about Tom, whom everyone liked. But she wouldn't give in.

Aunt Claire was never divorced, I'd thought, but found out differently in her obit. My father's brother was her second husband … and yes, he too had been married once before meeting Claire. During wartime, he wrote letters to my father from a camp in Tennessee, waiting to fight the Germans or the Japs. The letters are full of getting-that-marriage-over-with, what to tell the lawyer, what not to tell.

Never divorced was Aunt Lillian, my only-child mother's favorite of the many Terrills she had to deal with. ("Lillian has *sense*," my mother said emphatically, implying that the others perhaps didn't.) Lillian and my father aside, the Terrill family tree had undergone much pruning in my father's generation. There were four (or five?) divorces among the six siblings.

Not a great deal of reaching toward the sun, either, on that family tree: Cousins were few, only eight of us the products of these six elders. We were divided generationally between the "older cousins" and the "younger cousins." I was the youngest, the only born after mid-century; my eldest cousin was born in the year of the stock market crash, 1929. I thought of him as simply another uncle.

The result of it all was that kids were outnumbered by adults at the loud and loudening family parties, where adults didn't much believe in "not saying it in front of the children." Politics, religion, sports, workplace or family gossip—their concerns were ours before we understood, and we grew smart beyond our years. Most of the aunts and uncles started families late in their lives, and thus the gatherings became like history lessons or time machines: Their talk of "Ma" and "Pa," the grandparents I'd never known, who were born in the 1870s. Pa could pick up any brass instrument and play it, had a beautiful singing voice, played piano well. Ma could make a meal for the whole family on half a pound of ground chuck. Summers on Uncle Art's farm. Early Packards and Plymouths. My father born on the kitchen table of the family house a short walk from the depot where Pa was the station agent. Grandfather Terrill "played around," my mother contended, though she'd never met him in the flesh. By the end of her life, "Ma" was addicted to morphine, a victim of crippling arthritis. All true? Someone's faulty memory at work? As a child I knew only that I was not to question what was said. Just listen, and listen we kids did.

And their bizarre cousin Ray who, the story goes, donned a fake mustache and bad toupee, took the train out of and back into town, and lit a warehouse on fire to collect the insurance money. He did time, but the family laughed about the incident years later, as they laughed about most things. I met Ray only once when he drove from Chicago for the weekend to visit. Strapped on the top of his purple, ten-year-old Cadillac that leaked oil in our driveway, was a mattress. He had a bad back.

Years later still, I drove my brother to an Ohio archive for his genealogical research. One mid-nineteenth century Terrill, maybe in our line and maybe not, had been hanged, a newspaper account read, on questionable evidence. But, the item concluded, since he was an undesirable character, the town "did not consider it much of a loss."

If our forebearers are our fate, mine is a mixed legacy. But the aunts I knew placed the family in a better light. Their actions and independence pre-dated feminism. Was it something in the gene pool? Or just stubbornness and self-certainty that led to those divorces before the culture had said that they were okay? The aunts did what they wanted, said what they thought, more Barbara Stanwyck than Donna Reed, less Doris Day than Billie Holiday— whom, white and coming of age in the twenties, they must have liked much less. Their attitudes toward race were, sadly, those of their times: "Well, I guess *some* of them are all right," allowed Aunt Mildred during the height of Civil Rights. It was a cliché of the day, and we'd hear it elsewhere as well, not to be repeated since my mother sympathized with the plight of "the Negro," as the usage of the sixties had it. Aunt Vivian probably said and thought worse—she who'd never met, never spoken to a black person, but who seemed to grant tolerance nevertheless toward those in the defensive backfield of the Green Bay Packers, our hometown team.

Hard as it is to imagine now, they passed their lives in an all-white world. The only black people they ever met were the deferential waiters on the train to Chicago. Had they the advantages of my generation, I think they would have spoken a language more native to their generous hearts.

And what to make of this anecdote, which I heard only once, I can't remember from whom: my father, on one of his frequent business trips to

Chicago for the railroad, accompanied after cocktails and dinner by the men of the other rail lines: the Missouri Southern; Rio Grande; Gulf, Mobile and Ohio. The group passed a small and peaceful civil rights demonstration on a street in the Loop. My Dad impulsively joined the end of the march and pretended to be one of the protesters. I can imagine him lifting his legs high, exaggerating his steps, and then looking back at his southern colleagues, knowing he would get their goats. He must have laughed at their disdain. Ever the jokester, a trait I know I've inherited, did he see more than the humor in his action? I like to think so, that he sensed something wrong with the way the southern men talked and what they seemed to believe.

✳

I had no sisters, and at family gatherings the house seemed full to me with these women not my mother. I remember especially the old house of Aunt Lillian and Uncle Bill, big and white and high ceilinged, with furniture that had seemed to me somehow fancier than other people had, though I think now it was probably just older. There was a bedroom right off the living room, something I'd never seen anywhere else; a bar set up in one corner of the living room was something I was considerably more familiar with. And there was Uncle Bill's sunroom, west facing toward the river, and set off to the right as we entered the place. There he read his newspaper, feet on stool, and smoked his wonderful and fragrant cigars. He had a television that actually had a remote control, linked by a cord to the set. When we all walked in for his surprise retirement party, he hardly looked up from his throne. Aunt Vivian asked, "Aren't you surprised?" His newspaper frozen at arm's length, Bill answered with his squeaky stutter, learned from an overly strict Germanic father. "I'm s-s-so surprised I don't know what to say."

While we all rooted for the Packers of that Lombardi era, Negro players and all, Uncle Bill had actually played for the Packers... but that was *before the existence of the NFL*—before even World War I. It was part of that ongoing history lesson. Bill had been a high school classmate of Curly Lambeau, and years later I pored through the archives at the Packer Hall of Fame to find the publicity shot of Bill in a three-point stance at guard, Lambeau behind him under center. Uncle Bill was nearly as much fun as the aunts.

During the Cuban missile crisis, I imagine most families avoided discussion of nuclear war until the children were in bed. Not the Terrills. Aunt Mildred was aghast at the rumors she'd heard about Civil Defense and evacuation protocol when the bomb was about to strike. "What happens," Aunt Mildred voiced to my parents, aghast, "if they say Johnny goes to Appleton and Ricky goes to Marinette, and you should stay behind?" The directive, if it existed, was probably something like the one Brits followed, sending children out of London during the War. But she would have none of it.

"What worries me," Aunt Gladys countered, "is the establishment of a Communist spearhead in our hemisphere."

That's the way I remember the phrase: not Communist *beachhead,* like a foothold for an advancing army, but *spearhead.* Surely that's the way a nine-year-old heard it, not the way she misspoke. Or maybe the aunts saw it that way: Russian spears literally flying across the ninety miles to south Florida (where none of them had ever visited). Perhaps cold war paranoia was for them an extension of the insecurity in those early marriages, now played out on a world stage: ex-husbands coming home drunk, now become men with Russian accents marching down Walnut Street in little Green Bay, Wisconsin.

As a boy, was I frightened at the prospect of burning up in a nuclear fireball? Not as much as I was fascinated with the heat and fallout from this good conversation.

＊

"Why don't you marry him, Mildred!" the aunts implored again, another topic as contentious as the prospect of the end of the world. "No, I went through one marriage," Aunt Mildred insisted to the jury of her siblings. "I won't make that mistake again." And so large-boned Tom persevered, in our family's circle but out of Mildred's arms. I was too young to consider the celibacy that his role forced. I did take note, though, when Mildred reported that Tom was teaching her to drive. Mildred would be at the wheel, I was told, with Tom seated snugly behind her in his white Dodge Coronet (with the push button transmission).

"I know how to go and turn and stop," Mildred said. Even as a kid, I was afraid she'd learned the techniques in that order! Thankfully, Tom was big enough for his leg to wrap around hers to access the brake.

"Did you hear Mildred broke up with Tom?" Aunt Vivian reported excitedly one Sunday after church, but before the Packer kick off. She and her husband Uncle Virgil—the sweet working man with the easy laugh—visited almost weekly that fall. It was big news, but the break-up, like the threat from Cuba, turned out to be temporary. Soon enough those missiles were on boats back to the Soviet Union, and by the family Christmas, Tom would be back standing in the kitchen with the other uncles.

I loved being witness to that adult talk, sometimes about others in the clan, but more often about how far the Packers would get and how the Kennedy brothers were trying to control big business. About shares of AT&T, whether to hold or to sell ("What difference does it make?" Aunt Mildred cackled, "You're going to croak and lose it all anyway!") And there was talk about April finally giving way to May and the weather that led to trout fishing, berry picking, swimming, and later hunting at the family cottage—the most beautiful time. Food was also a topic addressed with a passion on par with world affairs: where, for instance, was the best place to get broasted chicken, Krolls or Schaeffer's? Or my dad's favorite and thus the only right answer, The Swan Club? "That's the place where for dessert they give you those *knee joints*," he liked to say. "Knee*caps*," my mother always corrected, knowing that my dad knew very well what they were called.

Dad couldn't let the opportunity for a joke go by. To my cousins and his sisters, Carleton Terrill, my father, was the most entertaining of the siblings. "Oh, that Carleton," Aunt Mildred would cackle about my dad's deadpan, Mildred flushed after one glass of sherry at a family party, "he's always more fun than a minstrel show." "*Minstrel* show!???" we laughed. Gear up the time machine.

My father, teamed with his brother and brothers-in-law, were a match for the aunts in unpredictability and humor, could outdrink them and were allowed to, yet never a harsh word or incident from booze or other cause. I see the uncles leaning like figures in a moving portrait, elbows on the bar and hands gesticulating, making points in air. I remember the most mundane of subjects being discussed with passion that other families would reserve for death and dismemberment. Restaurant chicken, second marriages, nuclear holocaust—nothing was worth not having an opinion on for the Terrills. Nothing merited anything less than overstatement: the most, the worst, the farthest from town. I grew up in one evolving hyperbole. And those opinions would be argued, with and without logic, with and without cocktails, till the same point of no resolve was reached. The fun was getting there. I don't remember the particulars of the talk as much as I remember its invigorating lack of subtlety, its vast modulations in pitch, how quickly it came to a humorous end without much decided or agreed upon.

✳

Aunt Gladys, the eldest and first divorced, died in 1964, right after the first Kennedy. We'd gone from church to Lillian's house that unbelievable Sunday when someone had murdered the President's murderer. Gladys by this time was always in a dressing gown, her face reduced to a cancerous skull. She had moved in with Lillian and Bill a few years before, and now they were taking care of her at the end. "Is Aunt Gladys any better today?" I asked, not yet eleven, and I had to be told that she wasn't going to get any better, a concept new to me. It was the first of the deaths of that generation, and the only for which we weren't allowed TV for the whole weekend after her Friday passing. The old school said that was the way of mourning, to show respect.

Aunt Lillian died in 1984, only three months after my father. My mother had been to the hospital that evening and remarked to me on the way to the funeral three days later how red had been the blood that Lillian had coughed up on the front of her hospital gown. In retrospect, it was a sign, my mother said. *In retrospect*: the kind of irony that death creates of the time just before it, when no one knew for sure. An aneurism, they'd diagnosed, and Lillian was too frail for the surgery they'd tried. I remember her just months before her passing, walking unsteadily from the family plot at the funeral of her younger brother, my father, and then being steadied on the arm of another mourner. I had seen one leaf settling into my father's open grave to rest upon the casket. That single leaf would never fall from my memory, emblem, I think, of the solitude of our passing.

Aunt Mildred, who never married Tom, (and never got her driver's license), had died three years before in 1981, dropped suddenly to the kitchen floor of her apartment, in that building with the one door and the many doors. Perhaps she'd arisen to answer the phone, getting up from one of her "shows." Those were her afternoon soaps. *"Oh, there's such fighting and sadness and drama, you know,"* said she whose later life had held so happily little of it. Mildred's heart broke finally and completely that one time, and she lay where they found her before suppertime. She left most of her money to the church and shares to each sibling, most of whom didn't need it. The entire family, working class and uneducated, knew how to pinch a penny and all left money behind.

Tom had gone on providing that apartment for Mildred in the big rental house he owned. I think he owned it just so he could do so. He charged her not enough rent to cover even utilities, my mother said, and was almost as generous to the other tenants, whose rent I'm sure he never raised. "As long as Millie has a place to stay," he said to us again and again, perhaps hoping we'd make his case with her, and we never did, and it wouldn't have mattered. When Mildred died, Tom's letter to my mother, in the garbled hand and with the bad grammar of his grade school education: "I can't believe that God has taken Millie I ask myself why oh why, why oh why. What ever will I do?"

He carried that torch till he died. Not so much a flame as a dim but steady glow like the giant lighted milk bottle atop the Fairmont Dairy on Broadway where Tom had worked the night shift. We looked for it whenever we drove past: a giant milk bottle always appearing as a surprise to a boy far too young to drive and who thus held no sense of geography in his own hometown. What lay beyond Norwood School and Herman's candy store? *There's the big milk bottle. See?*

Aunt Vivian died in the early 90s, still not tired of life, her second (or third) husband passed away, still smoking even after her circulation left her hands permanently like ice. Still making her great pies, crusts flakey with sugar and lard, when I went to visit her those last years. I had met Linda by then, and Vivian—the woman so suspicious of those she imagined different from herself—was anxious to meet her, but died before we could arrange it. Vivian knew Linda was Chinese and made no mention of it, either because she knew it wasn't an issue for me or, what I prefer to believe, because it wasn't an issue for her.

Even near the end Vivian walked daily the long road around the lake where she lived in a trailer home across from her one son. "In her coffin," my mother told me, "she looked like she was about to get up and dance." She'd been a good dancer, and had still gotten up some holidays to jitterbug solo to Ted Weems while my father gazed wistfully toward the ceiling and wished those days were back again.

Years later my brother visited Aunt Claire, who like my mother stayed married the balance of her husband's life. Claire had no memory of my father, her brother-in-law whom she knew for forty years until his death. "Claire is in even worse shape than Mom," my brother wrote me. His note was enclosed with his half of the pay for the woman we'd hired to help our mother with housework and shopping, help her remember who she was, and sometimes who other people used to be.

"What did your dad die of?" my mother asks me during a visit.

"Mesothelioma … the lung lining."

"So it was cancer then?"

And another time, the Alzheimer's progressing, as the loneliness of her shrinking world seeps in: "Your father should have hung around a little longer."

It must be like an apartment building, I think, that loneliness and not knowing what is going to happen, not knowing why the world is going away. Only one door is the door home in the vacant and anonymous hallway.

※

I think of the aunts now as a set, apart from the trajectory of their individual past lives, about which I knew much less. They are a sister act, as if in vaudeville, dressed alike for the performance. All are talking at once, and too loud. All are agreeing, yet seeming to disagree. Or I imagine them in a row of seats in a studio audience for some TV show of the day, *The Best of Groucho* or *Hollywood Palace*, all smiles and applause.

. I find in dusty boxes in my closet, snapshots of the aunts as pleasant-looking young women. Women in flapper's dresses, very round hats, standing next to the cars I've seen in gangster movies, cars with running boards, parked sometimes in front of country roadhouses or dance halls. The shots are black and white, or sometimes hand tinted color. And on each the unlined, unmarked smiling face of someone I think I recognize.

The past is marked for each of us by what we didn't know that we now do. I didn't know how much I loved them: the aunts asking always how school was. Aunts exclaiming what was wrong with the Seventh Day Adventists Mildred was becoming interested in. Aunts cooking too much food and urging us to finish it. Aunts picking raspberries and making pie, finding just a handful of wild blueberries at the edge of the property near the wet, tall grass, and then giving them to me to try, so sour, but the taste so real, so unlike cereal or pancakes or things from the store.

Aunts who came with us to the beach, posing for a picture, standing behind us in bathing caps, hands over the shoulders of each of the nephews, my brother and me. Aunts watching *Gunsmoke* and *Your Show of Shows*. Aunts reading *Son of the Grand Eunuch* and *Saratoga Trunk*. Aunts paging through *Argosy* or *TV Guide*. Aunts shushing us to hear the weather report—from that guy who mumbles so on the radio broadcast.

Aunts stating their opinions: unfounded opinions, certain opinions, ideas to top other ideas, some bad but forgotten easily. Laughter to top laughter. Maybe one more cocktail. Aunts lighting cigarettes, aunts lighting charcoal, aunts lighting our simple three-room cottage where we stayed summer weekends, piled up like the crew of a submarine.

When the red light goes on, aunts speaking into the new reel-to-reel tape recorder my brother and I got for Christmas that very morning. It's a moment they intuit may be remembered. "Johnny and Ricky...Merry Christmas and Happy New Year," and then the dog lets out a loud bark and everyone laughs and includes her in their best wishes.

Two Stories

Spring Creek

TROUT FISHING HAS BEEN POOR THIS YEAR. ON OUR USUAL STREAM, THE water was too high, then it was too low. Maybe last winter was too harsh. Maybe too many fishermen this spring.

Now it's near the end of fishing season, late September. My older brother John and I are camped on a secluded lake, and today we're hoping to fish the Weirgor, with the promise of better water levels and a stream that's not plagued by whatever is bothering the other ones around here.

We want to fish the spot where Spring Creek joins the Weirgor—but first we have to find that spot. Years ago, during a hot Memorial Day weekend, we backpacked in, camped on high ground above the Wiergor. But we found that to get from there to the confluence with Spring Creek would have meant a tough hike through swamp, brush, and alders. As far as I can remember, we never even tried to make it. I say "remember," because that camping trip was a while back—about forty years back.

Today we decide simply to hike along Spring Creek until we hit the juncture with the Weirgor. Then after we catch our limit of trout, *maybe* we can try to find that campsite—if we're crazy enough—just for old time's sake.

We start into the woods along Spring Creek on something that looks like it might have been a logging road once upon a time, now overgrown. Soon the vestiges of tire tracks give way to something you might call a "path." Then a deer trail, intermittent. After that, just woods. But if we keep Spring Creek on our right, eventually we will get to the confluence.

It's a perfect fall day, sun and clouds, the first leaves turning. Sixty degrees, low humidity, a steady breeze we can hear passing above in the hardwood canopy and through tall white pines. "This is kind of fun" I say. "Kind of an adventure." What I mean is, at least we have a reason to do this hike—which makes it better than fishing and not catching anything.

I'm leading the way, John lagging a bit behind. We stop every once in a while for him to catch his breath. This is due to his condition—about which I'm going to tell you only that, barring a car accident or plane crash, something that could befall any of us, he knows what he's going to die of. Not many of us can say that, even at his age of 72. He complains now about what he's lost, but I'm more impressed by what he can still do. We're tramping through the woods, uphill and down. There's no trail, and except for the rest stops I don't see that he's hiking much slower than either of us used to.

Forty minutes in we stop to reconnoiter. It's already farther to this confluence than we thought we'd have to walk. Thus neither of us brought water. My phone doesn't work out here, so it's back in the car. John has brought a Garmin that he found in the woods last year. There's no map loaded. But following the Creek, why would we need a map? We can't possibly get lost.

"The Garmin says we've walked .43 miles."

"That's crazy" I say. "We've gone much farther than that."

Then we figure out that the Garmin is telling us how far we are *from* the car, measured as the crow flies. (I've always wondered, just who is this crow, and why is he always telling you you haven't gone as far as you think?) We've been meandering with the creek, going from southeast to southwest.

"If this weren't such a nice day," one of us says, "you know we wouldn't be doing this." The other agrees.

"I doubt I'll be doing this in two years," John says. I'm still impressed he's doing it at all. The doctor gave him a range of life span when he got his diagnosis. He's passed the lower number. But every case is different, the doctor said.

"I won't be doing this in two years, either." I say, out of breath myself. "Because I'll be smarter."

I'm starting to get thirsty—mostly from the walk, but partly because that last, unnecessary drink I had the previous night around the campfire has left a taste of cotton in my mouth. I reach in my pocket for a stick of gum.

Damn, only one left. I tear it in half.

We're at that point in a journey where you know where you're going, but you don't know where you are. The destination should come anytime now. Dare you turn back? Dare you leave yourself open to regret?

"That clearing up ahead should be the Weirgor." "See that light through that stand of birch? "Over that next rise?" "…where the creek bends sharp to the south?"

We've tramped through the woods eighty minutes now. "The Garmin says we've gone .54 miles," John says.

"Total bullshit!" I say. "You should have left that thing in the woods where you found it."

"Even if we find the stream now," I go on, "we'll be too tired to fish it. And we'll still have to walk all the way back over an hour, plus however much more we walk to find that campsite from 1981. Or 1881, or whenever it was."

We stop. It's a perfect spot for a long rest. Of course, the Weirgor may be only just out of eyesight. Always just out of eyesight. We're on a ridge, high above Spring Creek, seated on a conveniently placed fallen maple. The temp is cool, but not cold. Jacket weather. The Creek has picked up a little more flow from runoff and is falling over rocks and the roots of trees. There isn't much wildlife in dense forest, but a kingfisher is flicking from branch to branch above the water. A red squirrel pokes its head out of the brush, then scurries off, surprised to see us. I can't imagine anybody has walked here. Maybe ever.

This rise offers what passes for a vista in the woods in Wisconsin. The same thing in every direction: trees, lots of them. But it's beautiful.

"If a guy had a heart attack here, can you imagine trying to get him back?" John says. "You could just leave him here." I agreed, the spot was that nice, so nice that it turned out to be our destination. Neither of us said so, but we wouldn't be going any further.

"A guy could do worse," I add.

"You can bring my ashes here," John says.

I'm glad he's joking. Mostly because I could never find this spot again. What's more, I know he bought a cemetery plot back in town years ago.

So we turn around and as is always the case, the way back is faster. We're able to get back to the car in a little less time than it took us to get where it ended up we were going.

✳

Soon it's our last day after our last night of sleeping in the woods, when anyone would be tired and sore and smell bad. John has some commitment back in reality, and since I don't, I'm going to go out in my kayak one more time and fish the lake at which we we've been camped, while John packs up his gear to drive home.

We come to the woods for solitude—like Thoreau I guess—as much as for the fish. So John and I never camp in a campground, but instead have a few secret spots where we can be the only ones around. Most years we camp twice, spring and fall, avoiding the summer high season with its crowds and mosquitos. This year, we've gone twice as often, two times in spring and two times in fall, because we don't know how much longer we can make these trips. Trout fishing and being outdoors is one of the few things we have in common. We may not see each other during the long winter to come. There simply wouldn't be anything to do.

John strikes his tent and drives off without word, since we've already taken leave. I'm too far out on the water to as much as wave. Now, after several days of small talk, everything is eerily quiet. I take another cast. There's a stillness on the water and on the shore, so that I can hear my lure disturb the silence when it hits the surface of the lake. A loon across the water makes no sound.

I'm struck by a chill of recognition. A time would come when I would be coming here alone. Or would I not come at all? A further time would come when our favorite campsite would be empty of either of us—the way it looks now from the water—neither of us able to return. Too old, too sick, passed on. Maybe just too lazy. I had always known that was the case, because how could it not be? But suddenly I am *aware* of it, the *real* of it, in the front of my brain, resting just above my eyes.

Before John drove away, I saw him stand at the shore and pause for a moment to look out, I suppose at the autumn colors, the lake and the sky, each a reflection of the other. The sun was shining now after two days of cloudiness—shining the way it always seems to be just about the time one has to pack up to go home. The end of the season making fools of us all.

✳

Interval: The Lesson

"You write too often in the elegiac mode," my friend Barry told me, years ago. At that moment, he was making me breakfast more or less one-handed while cleaning up the kitchen with the other hand, and all the while holding one of his infant twin sons. This couldn't have been possible. But the very attempt at it seemed like a judgment—his life in the vital present versus my grim celebration on the page of what was passing or had passed.

Thirty-five years later, what Barry said about me is still true. Why would it not be, older now as I am, with all those years to practice my dark attitude, and get good at it? Had the years of experience made it any easier for me to age? Hard to say. Had I really been writing my own elegy all these years? Convenient if you want to control how you might be remembered.

But that doesn't seem to be at the heart of the matter. I don't mind much the thought of not existing, though I imagine it may be tough to say goodbye. What I most want, selfishly, is for the things around me to remain even if I'm not there with them. Like I want that campsite, seen from the lake, to still be there. I mean this for the natural world, could care less about the car wash where I worked in high school, etc. etc. I know I tell people this all the time. The elegiac mode can be redundant as well. Ask me.

"You can't take it with you," the old expression chides. But it should also say that you can't know how much or how little will be left behind. That's the hard part.

✳

The Bear

The second story begins before I was left alone on that lake, but after our boondoggled excursion down Spring Creek. We're bushed from the hike, and I'm looking forward to lunch and a beer, and then a delightful nap. We get back to our isolated campsite and I see parked away from our tents and near the lake, two ATVs with kennels mounted on the back. Bear hunters. I can hear the eight caged hounds crooning, and the flat yellow staticky sound of the hunters' walkie talkies, like in a crime scene. An electric sound, water sprayed on a brick wall. There goes my solitude. John lives in these parts so I'm not sure it matters as much to him as it does to me, city mouse that I am.

Bear hunting is a sport in which a gaggle of hunters will release dogs with radio collars through the woods on the scent of a bear that, sometimes, they've baited with old meat. This time of year, with the thin air of fall, you can hear the pack for miles around. The hunters tear up and down the dirt roads and trails in their ATVs to follow the pack's progress, and when the dogs have treed a bear, the hunters walk the shortest distance they can through the woods, and one hunter is elected to shoot the cornered animal.

"The bear bait explains that dead smell last night," I say to John. But he says they don't always use bait if they're using dogs. "It still stunk," I add.

The hunters' ATVs are mud splattered. "Potter Family," a wooden sign reads, affixed to the back of one of the kennels. A Trump campaign sticker, from the first election, is faded to white on the other. Now a truck with a trailer, and an SUV have joined them, all clustered in our campsite a half mile from the main road.

"Sorry for the interruption," one man says, the one in the truck. He's meaning to be polite, and succeeding at it, upsetting my attempt at typecasting.

"They shot the bear over on that island, and they went to bring him back in a canoe. It shouldn't take a super long time."

Soon the canoe lands and the party gather around. I count thirteen hunters in all, including two teen girls in new, bright-colored stocking caps. One wears a sweatshirt that reads, "Bear Hunters Association." It's a weekday, and they're skipping school. The rest are men, looking older than they probably are in a way common to people in these parts, where life has been none too easy in recent years. Small towns, too, are dying.

John is trying to chat with one of the older hunters, maybe a grandpa to the teen girls. Everyone is talking at once, laughing, excited. I'm standing to one side, a measured distance apart, as I often like to be from things, and I can make out only bits of what the hunters are saying:

Is the bear dressed?
We need to get a lighter canoe!
…About 200 pounds. That boy there shot a 500-pounder last year
Yup, the bear is dressed…
When the bear was treed it slapped down at the one dog bam bam *and*
that dog ran off as fast as all get out…
…we stopped and decided, do we want to shoot this bear?

Two men now drag the bear by its front paws up the rough dirt landing from the lake. As it passes me, I see the bear's closed eyes, the perfect snout, the deep, unbroken black of its fur, glistening.

The bear is bigger than a cub, probably a yearling. For some reason I notice most the smooth pads on its back feet. Perfect, they hold not a wrinkle, not a bit of rock or duff. The heel and the toes, perfect. The weight of the bear's legs draws two lines in the sand as the men get him to the vehicles.

Several of the men lift the bear high and it lands with a metal plunk in the back of one of the ATVs. At that moment, the hounds begin to all talk at once, and the sound of it grows louder, covering all the other talk and the sounds of movement, the canoe loaded on the trailer and car doors slamming.

Then slowly and for a long time, I can hear the baying of the hounds as the convoy makes its way further up the rutted road from the campsite.

Except for me, everyone in my family hunted. I know about these things. I know the DNR has studied the optimum bear harvest. John's not bothered by anything in the scene, tells me that his stepdaughter shot a bear just last season, or maybe it was the year before.

But when I saw the bear, so recently made lifeless, I needed time—time for what I was feeling to swim across a lake to meet my mind where it was camped, alone on a shore. I find, more often now, that I need these moments to collect myself, to collect pieces of experience, and to try them out this way and that way. To make *a sense* of it, one of many possible patterns. A reason. That bear looked as though it could get up any minute. It looked … fresh. Alive.

The next morning, I go out in my kayak hoping to inspect the island where the bear was shot. But I can find no good landing for my boat. I look from the water, but the island is small, unremarkable. A few cedar trees and dead snags. Grass. Reeds in the shallows. Like any other island.

Not long later I hear a pair of sandhill cranes, the washboard rattle of their cries. They're probably the ones I heard back at camp yesterday and the day before. It's time to migrate. I spot them now as they circle right above my kayak, so that I have to strain my neck to look, and almost tip. They circle again, higher. It's almost as if they see me here, take notice, but I know they don't. Then a third circle, still higher and I think that, maybe like loons, they're too heavy to fly off in a straight line. They must circle to gain altitude. When they reach the top of the thermal, the cranes will simply glide.

Their strange cry continues and grows weaker with each turn. They are higher and higher and are soon out of my sight.

About the Author ━━━━

Richard Terrill's essays have appeared widely in journals such as *River Teeth, Fourth Genre, Colorado Review, Missouri Review, Crazyhorse,* and *New Letters,* as well as in the collection *Fakebook: Improvisations on a Journey Back to Jazz. Saturday Night in Baoding: A China Memoir* won the Associated Writing Programs Award for Nonfiction. Terrill is also an accomplished poet. His three collections include *What Falls Away Is Always* (from Holy Cow! Press) and *Coming Late to Rachmaninoff,* winner of the Minnesota Book Award. He has been awarded fellowships from the National Endowment for the Arts, the Wisconsin and Minnesota State Arts Boards, the Jerome Foundation, the MacDowell Colony, and the Bread Loaf Writers' Conference, as well as Fulbright Fellowships to Korea, China, and Poland. He is Professor Emeritus at Minnesota State, Mankato, where he was a Distinguished Faculty Scholar, and currently works as a jazz saxophone player. He lives in Minneapolis. For additional information, please visit *www.richardterrill.com.*